# Building Critical Literacy and Empathy with

# Graphic Novels

# Building Critical Literacy and Empathy with

# Graphic Novels

Jason D. DeHart
The University of Tennessee, Knoxville

NATIONAL COUNCIL OF TEACHERS OF ENGLISH
340 N. NEIL ST., SUITE #104, CHAMPAIGN, ILLINOIS 61820
WWW.NCTE.ORG

*Staff Editor:* Cynthia Gomez

*Manuscript Editor:* Michael Ryan

*Interior Design:* Jenny Jensen Greenleaf

*Cover Design:* Adrian Morgan

*Cover Image:* iStock.com/seb_ra

ISBN 978-0-8141-0167-4; EPUB eISBN 978-0-8141-0168-1; PDF eISBN: 978-0-8141-0169-8

It is the policy of NCTE in its journals and other publications to provide a forum for the open discussion of ideas concerning the content and the teaching of English and the language arts. Publicity accorded to any particular point of view does not imply endorsement by the Executive Committee, the Board of Directors, or the membership at large, except in announcements of policy, where such endorsement is clearly specified.

NCTE provides equal employment opportunity to all staff members and applicants for employment without regard to race, color, religion, sex, national origin, age, physical, mental or perceived handicap/disability, sexual orientation including gender identity or expression, ancestry, genetic information, marital status, military status, unfavorable discharge from military service, pregnancy, citizenship status, personal appearance, matriculation or political affiliation, or any other protected status under applicable federal, state, and local laws.

Every effort has been made to provide current URLs and email addresses, but, because of the rapidly changing nature of the web, some sites and addresses may no longer be accessible.

**Library of Congress Control Number: 2023947583**

# Contents

# Introduction:
# Finding the Perfect Text

Perhaps one of the most prominent narratives among comics fans is the story of the childhood collection, carefully curated over time, which is then tossed into the garbage by an older family member. This "kids' stuff" story positions comics as readily trashable; another common story is the comic that contains adult themes and content, barred from young hands by a dutiful adult. Strange how stories of both simplicity and complexity can be applied to a single medium. I know these stories well as a long-time comics reader, as well as a passionate educator who has negotiated the question of whether or not comics "counted" in the English language arts classroom.

My answer is yes, and this book explores comics as literature that can allow for critical encounters and deep sense-making.

I also know the challenge of the hunt for the ideal reading material, both as a student and a teacher. High-interest texts were not a mainstay of my life as a student in the 1980s and 1990s. Indeed, comics and popular characters were quite sparse in my reading life at school and were often texts and worlds that I believed only suited my at-home time. The texts I loved most did not seem welcome at school. Instead, I played the "reading game" of engaging with texts at the level of answering questions at the end of chapters for assignments while missing as many days as I could to immerse myself in the stories I truly enjoyed.

As a middle school English teacher, from 2007 to 2015, I quickly found that many of my students readily engaged with comics. Once more, comics were not always present around the school building. I added titles to my classroom library, which were checked out often (and sometimes not returned, which I took as a compliment). In the move to higher-order, complex texts in 2012 in our school district, I found the rationale for including comics in my classroom to be a harder sell, as well as for including popular novels of the time like the Hunger Games series. The opinions about what counted as text, and what could be considered complex, were once more at the surface of conversation.

In this book, I contend that comics are actually quite complex, even in their simplest forms, and that these texts have much to offer teachers who work with students of all ages. I have worked with Dr. Morgan Blanton from Appalachian

State University and Dr. Shuai Zhang at The University of St. Joseph to begin exploring this issue further. Instead of seeing comics as "kids' stuff" or a lesser form of reading, I work to (re)position comics as complex and flexible texts that can apply to a wide audience, from early/emergent literacy to well into adulthood. I also embrace comics as texts that lead to criticality; by this, I mean they can allow for conversations about complex social and emotional concepts as well as exploration of ideas. Of course, in order to reach this level of interaction with the text, readers must take a critical stance.

In each chapter, I provide standards from *Learning for Justice* to link to what it can mean to be critical and thoughtful in classroom work, as well as ideas from scholars of both comics and critical literacy to return to these commitments to meaningful instruction. The texts I feature only help educators do part of this work—teachers must also be open to conversations about inclusive and welcoming environments and embody these practices while considering our own biases and responses to students and colleagues. I encourage readers to explore comics further as more and more texts are published.

## Positions and Pedagogy

Before delving into the background of how this book came to be, it might be helpful for me to note the larger philosophical foundation I work from: Simply put, I believe it is essential for readers to see themselves represented in texts, and I define "text" broadly to include film, digital media, and comics (Bezemer & Kress, 2015), among other forms. The idea of representation is far from original to me; it stems from Bishop's (1990) work on how texts can act as mirrors and windows, reflecting experience, offering a viewpoint into another person's life— and as sliding glass doors, providing opportunities for readers to walk through those doors and out into the world to enact change. I also note Stuart Hall's major contributions in regard to representation in film. In fact, my research path began with my love of film and comics.

In my work, I carefully select texts that foreground socially significant issues (Lewison et al., 2014) for students of all ages to engage with in their reading and writing, and I take the same careful approach to sharing texts with children (and adults) whenever the invitation arrives. I especially look for texts that lend themselves to exploring deeper questions about reality and experiences—without necessarily providing easy answers. Many of the writers I talk with have said that this pursuit of questioning is part of their work.

Reading from a *critical* stance not only expands literary understandings but also invites readers to examine critical issues and inequities tied to race, gender, income, and disability, among other intersections of identity (Bishop, 2016). Sometimes this process of text choice is an emotional one as teachers simultaneously search for the perfect text while recognizing there is never enough time to teach all of the books we would like to.

Comics and graphic novels are uniquely designed so that the idea of seeing one's self represented in a book or peering into someone else's life can reach new possibilities, both in words and images. Not only that but the audience and creator-base that has become part of the forefront of this medium has grown dramatically in the past decade.

Comics can be celebrated for their utility, and the titles I featured in this book are examples I have found to be particularly powerful from my practice as a teacher and teacher educator. If comics did not work for engaging students and building critical dialogue, I would find something else to use—and, as I will explore in the next section, these texts have been foundational in my own literacy development. From the beginning of my writing and scholarship, I have looked for ways to showcase the linking of theory and practice.

I have also seen, at times in classroom spaces and at other times in face-to-face and online clinical spaces, the possibilities for engagement that occur in the pages of comics and graphic novels that are not as immediately available in other types of books.

Graphic novels and comic books have become an increasingly welcome format for literacy development with students in elementary and secondary classrooms, but there is still work to be done in recognizing the potential and complexity of these books. Careful and well-planned teaching with graphic novels entails considering the best fits for students, bringing to mind Ohlhausen and Jepsen's (1992) "Goldilocks Principle." The goal in applying comics is not to replace *all* reading experiences with visual texts but to approach these books as yet another "go-to" for teachers who are seeking to engage students and encourage voracious reading.

When it comes to defining the term *graphic novel,* I turn to the concept of an extended text that works in a comic book-like format. Many view the term as a marketing phrase. I also recognize that sometimes, depending on the age of the students educators are working with, picture books may overlap with this definition. The term "comic book" is often used to refer to books that are somewhere around 22- to 48-page editions, and the words "floppies" have come into use at times among fans, demonstrating the flexible nature of these relatively short books. A graphic novel may include a collection of these shorter stories in anthologized form but may also be a term applied to a standalone story. The word "comics" refers to the nature of the medium itself, and I use it as often as possible to note that graphic novels are not the only type of comics that are worthy of attention.

Both the terms *comic book* and *graphic novel* entail a collaborative design of images and pictures that do not exist in separate spaces but that overlap as a series of panels, or small narrative boxes, as well as a host of other semantic and syntactic visual features (McCloud, 1994). Comics can be contrasted with traditional novels, which include text only, or picture books, which delineate text and images in spaces that are often separated. Because of these layers of meaning-making systems, comic book and graphic novel pages offer opportunities for analysis as well as possibilities for dialogue and creation.

Readers can note the grammatical features contained in visual stories. Scott McCloud (1994) unpacks the multiplicity of grammatical features that graphic novels include in his book *Understanding Comics: The Invisible Art.* In this book, I have made use of these terms to talk about the composition of the comics page as well as how these pages can be uniquely engaging for readers. Comics do have a grammar, and comics pages are replete with opportunities for further analysis.

One consideration for what constitutes a comic book or graphic novel may be the question: Does the text stand on its own in such a way that it can be separated from the images and still work in the same way as a narrative? This can also feel like splitting textual hairs, which is of little practical, educational value. What matters to me is that the students in my classroom become active readers and critical thinkers (see Figure 0.1 for questions that can foster this conversation).

Essentially, I recommend that teachers include and highlight reading practices with books that engage readers activity in thoughtful literacy processes, regardless of the nomenclature that surrounds those books. Comics have the

## What Does It Mean to Be Critical?
## Approach + Text

- How does the text itself work?
- What purpose am I setting?
- Do students have the opportunity to question?
- Do I pose a range of perspectives through the text?
- Is there sufficient time given to pausing and talking about topics that are part of the text?
- Do my students have the opportunity to talk about and process the text?

**FIGURE 0.1.** Questions to Encourage Active Reading and Critical Thinking

reputation of being too easy for some, and too edgy or mature for others—but, then, there is no single story of the comic book. Reading a wide range of comics can help in reconsidering what the medium has to offer.

## Text Showcase: When Stars Are Scattered

As part of collaborative teaching, I have centralized the work of Victoria Jamieson and Omar Mohamed in the graphic novel *When Stars Are Scattered*. This text from an authentic coauthor voice is a powerful and poignant story that offers a variety of avenues for exploring one refugee's life journey and the ways Omar Mohamed's narrative can be linked with a variety of experiences and questions about life. Jamieson crafts the visuals that convey Mohamed's story of survival in the camp, Dadaab, including his search for family, quest for a future, and care for his brother, Hassan. I try to prioritize texts as much as possible that offer readers insider perspectives as authentic stories. The book is a National Book Award finalist, earned a Middle School Honor for the Schneider Family Book Award, and was a YALSA Great Graphic Novel for Teens, among other awards and accolades. Even though it is drawn with almost cartoonish forms, the story is complex and can lead to probing questions.

The book has been a centerpiece in one of my favorite classroom projects, which culminated in a virtual author visit with Omar Mohamed at the end of the fall 2020 semester in a graduate class I was teaching. I worked with approximately 25 students to explore *When Stars Are Scattered*, and our talk was fruitful as we journeyed through this text and explored other window texts, which were presented through a collaborative web space.

Comics and visuals can be used to explore contemporary narratives, as well as to reconsider stories that have been around for a while. In Figure 0.2, I showcase illustrated work I did as I led high school students in a consideration of John Steinbeck's work. From Steinbeck to literature published this year, visuals and comics can be used as ways to encounter authors who share both insider and outsider perspectives.

**FIGURE 0.2.** Revisioning the Canon: A Comic Book Invitation with John Steinbeck's *Of Mice and Men*

Throughout this book, I offer a look at what works best in comics. I examine the components, possibilities, and limitations of each text and explore how I have used or might use these books as a teacher and teacher educator.

## Components

*When Stars Are Scattered* is a biographical/autobiographical collaborative narrative. Unlike an author's work like Steinbeck, the book takes on co-authorship in both words and images. It is also written from an insider perspective. The book's author, Omar Mohamed, shares his story as artist Victoria Jamieson captures his childhood in Dadaab in panels and images. The book is designed in a way that is accessible and friendly yet explores very resonant themes of global awareness and empathy. This insight from an author's perspective is unique in an industry in which narratives have often been claimed and re-presented by outsiders who relay the stories *for* a firsthand experience or by those who fictionalize the story entirely.

Using this approach to the text as a model, I will focus on the aspects of the texts that work across communication forms, from words to images to designs.

## Possibilities with the Text

With a presentation that is both welcoming and even cartoonish yet conveys complex issues, *When Stars Are Scattered* is an ideal text for beginning conversations about a range of topics with young readers. I have worked with teachers who, in turn, want to build literacy experiences with children from elementary ages all the way to high school. Graphic novels allow teachers a flexibility when considering the texts that students can build common lessons around. A book like *When Stars Are Scattered* can not only be used to explore further invitations to dialogue about the content itself but can also be a connection point to finding additional texts and themes that can lead to inquiry-based work and a deeper way of approaching literacy across content areas. With this in mind, students can experience the text and all it has to offer and then generate their own questions and topics to locate further reading opportunities.

As I explore texts throughout the chapters in this book, I begin with positive approaches in mind and consider what the text brings. Kylene Beers has suggested that books are written to be loved before they are ever part of an instructional plan. What is it that the book brings to the classroom? How do authors and illustrators stand with us as educators, ringing their voices in classrooms when our experiences fail to link to critical questions?

## Limitations

In addition to what the text brings, I note the critique that there is no one singular approach that connects with all readers. Talking about what a book lacks is never a fun process for me as I attempt to approach work from an asset-based frame. However, I do recognize that some authors' approaches fail to connect to critical topics, and I recognize that no single book can do all that I need it to. As I consider limitations, I will discuss how approaches and features in books may be missing. I will also share ideas about how to locate texts that work especially well.

For example, I note that some connections to critical issues are not as visible as others. I see *When Stars Are Scattered* is one text that can lead to rich dialogue around critical issues with additional texts in a kind of reading constellation. Reading widely is a must, and this includes graphic novels, picture books, and other types of works. Readers may instantly connect with one aspect of the story told in *When Stars Are Scattered* and may need to engage in additional questioning and conversation to appreciate additional parts of the story.

In the final analysis, I am most interested in books that inspire my students to continue reading

**FIGURE 0.3.** Student-Created Example (Writing What's at Hand/in Life)

and to create their own visual- and word-based product (see Figure 0.3 for an example of this).

## Steps in Instruction

In keeping with the education-centered and student-centered heart of this book, each chapter contains notes from my own practice about the ways I have engaged with students over the course of more than fifteen years to read and create comics. I include steps for instructional ideas in the chapters, including approaches to writing and composing.

As a next step in instruction from comics images, I suggest inviting students to discuss what counts as reading and what counts as a text. While students may not be ready to respond to this question immediately, offering multiple examples of texts that you, as the teacher, consume might be a first step in helping students recognize that they are already readers. It is my hunch that our students are reading constantly, but that the kinds of reading they are doing often do not fall within the educational hierarchical definition of what counts as reading. Instead of ignoring what is already an active process, I argue that educators (including myself) should engage students in these practices and connect them to classroom instruction, building natural and meaningful invitations to read and write whenever possible.

## A Road Map for the Reader

In this book, I will unpack graphic novels and comics in three ways. I first note that the audience for these books is fairly wide and diverse. Henry Jenkins, in the 2020 book *Comics and Stuff*, noted that the stereotypical comics audience is adolescent white males. From my work with comics, combined with my personal appreciation of them, I know that there are many more hands that take up graphic novels both as readers and as creators. Ideas about audience lead to a conversation in section one about using comics for reading and writing instruction. Do they, in fact, work as quality texts for instruction, or are they just eye candy? We will delve into that question together.

Following this look at audience, I explore the applications of graphic novels not simply as superhero narratives or pop culture stories but as ever-changing reservoirs that can provide a glimpse into human experiences. In this section, I look at how authors and artists in comics speak to issues of race, gender, ethnicity, and ableness, among other aspects of identity and experience. I share reading recommendations with eagerness in this section and again suggest that readers not only check out the books that I note but continue reading even more.

Finally, I conclude with a graphic novel teaching creed and some parting notes for why these texts are so important and relevant in our world now, as well as additional ideas for teaching applications in the third section. A podcast called *Words, Images & Worlds* has become one of my passion projects for sharing about authors and artists. The podcast is available on Spotify and Amazon, and some content is also available on YouTube. Because of these connections with authors and artists, I have, when possible, invited the creators themselves to share some words about their work throughout these chapters. This is both my way of showing appreciation for these creators and my step toward honoring the authentic voices that are part of these works—I am limited in my personal experiences, but I stand with an armada of literary voices whenever I teach about texts.

I have made wonderful and warm connections with many of these creative voices, and it is my pleasure to share them in this text as primary leaders in composing and creating opportunities with students. I have also included the work and words of former students who have agreed for their voices to be part of these chapters as well.

In this project, I acknowledge the insights of two literacy professors, Dr. Beth Buchholz and Dr. Beth Frye at Appalachian State University. The Doctors Beth, as I refer to them, have spent hours talking with each other about comics and graphic novels and sharing some of their insights with me. I have also co-taught linked courses in a variety of ways and contexts with these two scholars. Their architecture is evident in this book in the organizational structure of the overall book itself, as well in the organizational features of chapters. They have also provided helpful insights into the world of teaching using K–3 graphic novels, an aspect of this literature that I needed to learn more about in this process. While they did not engage as coauthors, their contribution is greatly appreciated in the overall design of this book.

## A Final Word

Since I began writing this book, a number of graphic novels and comics have been published. With more on the way, I conclude this introduction with a call to readers to keep reading widely and keep supporting creators. Many more voices need to be celebrated, and many more stories should be shared.

# Positioning
# the Works

# The Possibilities of Visual Narratives for Text Ladders and Literacy Work

ow do we, as teachers, engage younger and older readers who are striving? Do comics have any value for the reader who is skilled but who continues to be reluctant? My friend and one-time dissertation chair, Stergios Botzakis, has written about how comics can be used in undergraduate-level instruction, while Chase et al. (2014) have written about the powerful role of comics with K–2 readers. This is quite a span of possibilities with many titles in between the ends of this readership spectrum.

In my work with college students, I have highlighted the possibilities of text ladders for working with children when practicing literacy assessments. I emphasize the structures comics offer for engaging, supporting, and challenging readers. Based on this teaching, I have had students return to me with stories of success in having children who do not readily pick up books begin to devour graphic novels and express curiosity about them when they see them in classroom spaces.

These anecdotal responses are another piece of evidence supporting comics for literacy work that meets standards and enlivens instruction, and I am reminded of the second-grader who was immediately interested in a *Science Comic* (published by First Second) when I conducted a classroom visit in fall 2019. The second-grader noticed the book I was holding and then ran to the other side of the room, grabbing a comic that he loved from the classroom book bin and bringing it over to show me. I cannot think of a clearer example of what happens when people of any age love a book—they want to show others, tell others, and then find more books that recapture the reader experience.

With these connections in mind, I focus on the meaning-making that is part of interacting with words and pictures and call attention to steps teachers can take to keep engaging in the practice of recommending more books. When I consider graphic novels as flexible texts, I think about the enormous audience range and contend that graphic novels are, in fact, "real" books. To that end, these are not books on their way to becoming "real books." Such a Pinocchio approach to comics fails to appreciate what comics are and what they can do. Instead, the boundaries around who is interested in comics can be quite stretchy, as demonstrated in Figure 1.1.

## What Do Comics Offer?

- Stories through scripting in cinematic ways.
- The use of images and visual features.
- Elements of design.
- Simultaneous attention to multiple methods of storytelling.
- (En)visioning of experiences and fantastic possibilities.
- Individual and collaborative artistic work.

**FIGURE 1.1.** A Partial Summary of Comics Applications

## What's Complex about Complexity?

In my work with students, one of the points I emphasize is that texts exist on a ladder, and complexity is not easy to determine. "It depends" is a phrase that applies to many texts. Even with a prose-only passage, teachers must consider both the qualitative and quantitative demands of texts. By quantitative demands, I mean the length of words, kinds of words used, length of the overall text, and anything else that can be counted and measured. A number of systems have been employed for reaching measures like this, including Lexile levels and Flesch-Kincaid scores.

On the other hand, qualitative demands include the challenging content, sensitive issues, and emotionally complex material that books sometimes focus on. While a traditional ladder assumes movement upward in something like a progression along a perceived continuum of complexity, I see explorations of graphic novels (and all books) as a more free-form ladder, perhaps even a geometric one, operating in a double helix that allows students to go back and forth between examples of texts, moving beyond assumed levels of complexity. Sometimes rereading is the best reading to do while other times considering a book with more background information or a specific type of content knowledge is positive practice.

These measures of complexity sometimes lead to unique conclusions, as when a Kurt Vonnegut novel is placed at the fourth-grade reading level through a measure of the text complexity—usually determined through the length of words and sentences as well as the frequency of words. As it happens, many of the words and phrases, including the swear words that Vonnegut used, have a relatively accessible Lexile measure. Moreover, Vonnegut frequently used illustrations in his work. Anyone who has read Vonnegut knows how acerbic his writing can be, as well as the adult-oriented themes that he explored in both words and images. His work is certainly not "easy."

In a similar vein, a teacher might conclude that a character like Marvel's Moon Knight, the subject of a Disney Plus series, might be accessible to young people based on the popular nature of the character and potential readability results in graphic novels. However, many of the more recent titles that feature this character contain a level of violence that would make them a mismatch for young readers. In fact, many comics are more appropriately written and designed for older readers.

Let us consider what makes comics potentially complex. Think of the first time you read a comic book (or try one out before reading farther). If you are like me, your eye probably gravitates to the written word first. This is the hierarchical nature of the text, and it is the way that children have been taught to read. A shocking confession: Even as a comics reader for over thirty years, I still gravitate to the words. Sometimes, I read a comic quickly and reach the end, realizing I did not pause to take in the rich world-building that visually happens on the page. In this case, I travel back through the text and recognize that my understanding of the story, were I to just focus on the words, is incomplete. My eye goes from word to image, from background to foreground, from word bubble to word bubble. My understanding is cumulative as I take in all of what the page offers me, and the comics page is ideal for rereading.

These pauses to revisit what is on the page and build conversation about what is happening both within and between panels are part of where the complexity in comics lies. There is great comprehension work to be done with these books, and educators must also not immediately discount the frequency of Tier 2 and Tier 3 words in these texts. As comics creator Jerry Craft has pointed out, Marvel Comics as one example of the medium contain a variety of scientific terminology. Based on all of this, a text ladder for graphic novels would probably allow for movement back and forth, side to side, and laterally, in the same way that I just described the reading process in comics.

Again, who is the "right" reader for comics? It depends.

## Exploring a Master of the Comics "Hook"

I love it when I find a text that can hook readers, which can then lead to further engagement with literacy across a series of books—and sometimes even books contained in their own series. As reading teachers, we know the times that we have found what we consider to be the perfect book, a text and author we love, only to find that our students dismiss it.

One author who has demonstrated a mastery at the art of the series book for years and across multiple approaches is Dav Pilkey. A glimpse at this creator's prolific list of publications is a text ladder in and of itself. Sharing Pilkey's work with children is a marvel to behold, and I have witnessed firsthand how his work captures readers across assumed audience barriers. In school visits, I have found his books occupying the desks of fourth graders and middle school students alike.

Pilkey's work has an element of humor, playful revision, and whimsy, all presented alongside a subversive play with traditionally assumed teaching and writing structures. According to the author's own story, he was the student who was put in the hallway by teachers. This is an author whose very story celebrates the kid who might not necessarily find the kinds of books they are looking for in the traditional classroom library selections, and he is at once a master craftsman and an artist/author who does not seem to take himself too seriously. At the same time, he takes on serious questions, as when he presents the "refocus" form in the first *Dogman* graphic novel. I chuckled the first time I read this section, as I had seen similar approaches from teachers and similar responses from students who subverted the questions on the form.

While *Dogman* has satiric and potty humor appeal, in this chapter I concentrate on Pilkey's growing series of books, *Cat Kid Comic Club*. While some attention is given to gross-out humor in these books, the central focus is on a group of young characters who have formed a comic club and are engaged in making. Their interactions with each other and with text hold possibilities for talking about the kinds of experiences children have in and outside of writing classrooms on a daily basis. The chapter-by-chapter move from one type of writing and composing to another operates like a fun collection of mentor texts, with characters creating stories in comics and haiku form, as well as with Pilkey-imagined action figures (literacy play that was part of my childhood as well).

For components, the book has quickly become a series and, to be honest, I am not sure how Pilkey produces work as quickly as he does. While graphic novel/picture books have been a phenomenon, and while wordless comics will be explored later, *Cat Kid* is an example of an altogether different kind of fusion. It is as though Pilkey approaches each chapter to try something new stylistically.

In a clinic-based text ladder, I have used a wordless graphic novel, Aaron Blabey's Bad Guys series (explored in Chapter 4) and Pilkey's work to link with one another. I have alternated between *Dogman* and *Cat Kid*, but an exploration of Dav Pilkey need not be limited to these texts alone. From *Cat Kid*, I can travel with students to explore authors who fit into a grades 3–5 range, from Ben Hatke to Kazu Kibuishi to Jerry Craft. When I find an author, genre, or medium I love, I want to engage in further reading and exploration, and it is this kind of living and ongoing practice that I want to use to inspire readers of all ages. From the reading, I then explore steps in making (as seen in Figure 1.2).

Pilkey's work is a visual playground with traditional sketches, information on how to draw, and stories fashioned from the bones of action figures. His work brings to mind the ways children fashion stories out of toys, a topic explored by scholars like Karen Wohlwend who treat toys as tools for practicing literacy. Given the multitude of approaches, Pilkey's *Cat Kid* series immediately holds appeal for encouraging many individual styles. This approach lines up with Lynda Barry's note that bad drawings do not exist.

While Pilkey carries across a range of audiences, I recognize not all students (particularly older readers) might engage with his work immediately. It is the subversive nature of his ideas that might hold greater appeal for older readers, who have experienced school for some time.

**FIGURE 1.2.** Teacher-Created Illustration of Crafting Plot in Comics

## Comics and Literary Features

As demonstrated in the author-created example in Figure 1.3, comics have the potential to use both images and text to explore content. The natural scaffolding of this process, given the avenues to meaning-making that are woven into the texts themselves, lends itself to introductory narrative and creative work

**FIGURE 1.3.** Author-Created Comics Example
Using Literary Terms

as well as closer attention to literary features for analysis and evaluation. From my experiences, there is no state standard that cannot be explored and taught through the use of comics and graphic novels.

In short, I want to see students writing and creating in my classroom, using words, pictures, and a combination of the two. I want students to know that reading and writing are for them. In a classroom space, I envision (and practice) traditional paper approaches to drawing and creating, and there are increasing opportunities and tools for digital creating. This use of words plus pictures plus digital work can open up pathways for students who perhaps have never seen themselves as readers and writers to convey ideas and stories. As a challenge to myself, I have explored the English language arts state standards with comics in mind. I have taught in two states, and I think of both sets of standards when considering this work. I have attempted to apply each of the reading (literature) and reading (informational texts) standards to graphic novels. So far, I have not found a single standard that cannot be explored and mastered through the use of a comic book.

In order for children to see themselves as authors and creators, I suggest multiple opportunities to stop and write, draw, and create, and I encourage teachers to consider hosting author visits, including in-person and virtual meetings, to allow for encounters with creators who can speak into the lives of young children. I also do not limit this work to young children, as I have worked with adults who apply creative methods and digital tools to explore storytelling—steps which they can then share with others, including children in their classrooms.

I have always told my students that the world is our textbook. This world certainly includes comics—and more. Comics are part of that network of texts, and just because a text (or idea) is accessible does not mean it is necessarily simple.

# Invitations to Literacy

As I mentioned in the last chapter, as a kind of experiment, I have explored the English language arts standards with comics in mind. In this chapter, I am thinking particularly about reading. While some assume that graphic novels do not contain a wide range of words, there are numerous examples that suggest otherwise. I recommend reading comics published from 1950 to 1980, including popular titles in both the Marvel and DC universes. (As a sidenote, the cultural popularity of these books and the characters they feature is, in itself, a reason to consider including them to some degree in classroom instruction—readers will sometimes persist through difficult text if the subject matter is appealing).

Returning again to the point that Jerry Craft made about vocabulary in comics, the origin of many popular characters treats on scientific concepts (Spider-Man, the Hulk, and related characters, for example), as well as psychological concepts (Batman), interplanetary ideas (Superman and Martian Manhunter), and cultural and/or historical settings (Captain America and Wonder Woman). Concepts of ethnicity, race, and identity, as well as the political nature of these questions in the United States, surround characters like Sam Wilson/ Falcon, and teachers who are interested in featuring these characters can find immediate links to popular films. Even characters like Marvel's Hawkeye can be used to explore diverse abilities, given Clint Barton/Hawkeye's identity as a D/deaf character.

Just like our students, we as teachers can and should read widely. Without a full curation of the possibilities of comics, these texts may be seen as too limiting or too complex/adult, based solely on one or two examples and encounters. The many superheroes I have just mentioned only form one aspect of comics stories, but many types of graphic novels and comics exist, from K–2 examples to adult-themed graphic memoirs (see Howard Cruse's 1995 *Stuck Rubber Baby* as an example).

While comics can be used to tell fun and adventurous stories, stocked with humor and flashy characters, they can also take on social issues, tricky and nuanced questions, and global topics of social change and action.

# Intertextuality

Positioning comics as "real books" does not mean that other books and types of texts are pushed to the side. In fact, comics can be linked with prose novels, verse novels, and media-based texts, just to name a few. They can be the focal point of the lesson, material for individual reading time, or supporting text. The comics form can be used to fashion responses to traditional texts, as seen in the Figure 2.1.

Comics and graphic novels can be used to teach science concepts directly as a result of the focus they take, as seen in the work of Dallacqua and Peralta (2019) who examined the use of First Second's *Science Comics* in the classroom.

**FIGURE 2.1.** Student-Created Example of a Visual Character Representation (Inspired by *Race to the Sun* by Rebecca Roanhorse)

Imagine a text-based unit that begins with an introduction to a scientific concept through a text feature/graph. This notion of the visual can then translate to a comic book utilization of the subject before underpinning the foundations of the concept further by exploring a film clip or a real object. Finally, students can encounter the concept through the information in their science textbook, having built background knowledge through a variety of means and becoming experts on the topic through not one or two exposures to vocabulary and ideas but multiple examinations through multiple formats. This is also not to suggest that the science textbook offers the ultimate in reading experiences—this is just one example of how texts might layer with other texts in an instructional routine.

Sometimes a content area-connected response might not be connected with a text directed toward the subject matter. For example, after reading *Pawcasso* by Remy Lai and exploring content area connections that are made available through visual works, a student in one of my undergraduate methods courses created the image in Figure 2.2.

**FIGURE 2.2.** Ruthie's Comic Linking Science and Literacy

Though mostly wordless, save for "NOM" in Panel 2 and some additional language in Panel 3, the example could be used as a mentor text in its own right, paired with clips, textbook information, or additional visuals made available in the curriculum. Another direction I embrace with literacy is a close reading and focus on what the text brings. Reading panels closely, as I have illustrated, can be done with a focus on words. I also consider the artistic presentation of the images in storytelling. How did Ruthie introduce the topic in the first panel (top left)? Is there a main character in this mostly wordless story? Where is the story set? How does the main character change from panel to panel? In truth, I have previously spent the first ten minutes of a lesson examining a content-focused comic.

There are intentional choices that this student author made when composing this comic, and I can link this to the development of a story, the growth of a character, the importance of authorial decisions, the inclusion of necessary language, the decision to craft a particular title, and informational texts that can lead to further inquiry. In a classroom, the author and illustrator can then speak further to their creative decisions, linking a mentor text to a think-aloud.

What other cycles exist? How else can I view change in nature? What other processes of growth can I note? What processes of growth have I experienced? From a single page with four panels, an expert teacher can build inquiry, and a schema is ready to be constructed based on the visuals and the word-based components.

Chase et al. (2014), mentioned in the last chapter, advocate for modeling comics reading for students. Based on the work of Richard Allington, I suggest that modeling is an absolute must, regardless of content, students' age, or the scope of the lesson. Thankfully, teachers have accessible technology so that images in comics can be captured with document cameras or scanned and then displayed, illustrating for readers how to travel through the page, from panel to panel and word bubble to word bubble. As with films, teachers cannot necessarily assume that students will immediately make all of the connections they expect. Learning is always a modeled and active process.

## Invitations to Read Further

I am reminded of the student who asked what they can do for students who only want to read comics. Some students responded, "Let them read what they want." Others took the traditional approach of suggesting that comics were more like the junk food of the reading diet, and that children need more "solid" materials to digest in their reading lives (envisioning books this way leads me to strange mental images of the ways that the body responds to plant fiber found in book pages, by the way).

My response was that if a child only wanted to read comics, perhaps the teacher might consider what kinds of comics they like and recommend more complex ones as the child advanced in their reading. This solution does not position comics as "less than" but instead calls on the teacher to be a curator and to consider more examples to add to the classroom library. While this might not be the only approach I would take with the child in question, I now think back on the ways I learned to read. Flash cards and computer programs on 1980s machines were part of this, as were nighttime readings with my parents.

However, the first time I encountered an issue of *The Huntress* in 1989, I did not fully comprehend the implications of what happened in those comic panels and pages. I took a traipse along the pages, enjoying the depictions of characters, and picked up words where I could. I linked my thinking about this book with representations I had just seen in the 1989 Tim Burton *Batman* film. If you ask me about my reading history, it almost always includes a reference to this film and to a series of comics published by DC during this time.

From there, I read more and more comics. They were inexpensive and could be found occasionally in grocery stores and pharmacies. So, access was allowed and part of my daily life. There was also one graphic novel, an adaptation of *Clash of the Titans* (1981), in our school library. It was like the rose among thorns for me as a young reader, and my engagement with books was supported all the more. My schema had been built with popular film, and I was ready to tackle the ways that a story had been adapted by a writer and artist team. These literacy practices immediately led to comparing and contrasting works that was not prompted by a teacher.

While I was reading comics, I was entranced by the characters I loved, including Batman. Because of this love, I began exploring junior novelizations and even adult-aimed novelizations that featured the character. The books were most certainly beyond my reading level, but they captured my attention, and I worked through them, again gathering words wherever I could. Unlike *The Huntress*, they were not picture-heavy, but the images on the covers sufficed to whet my appetite for uncovering the content inside. More shared universe/licensed novels included Indiana Jones books and titles featuring comic and pulp characters.

Teaching is a creative and rich process, and I cannot imagine myself doing anything else. At the same time, reading is a complex and active process. To make the most of text, there is no one single approach. For years, reading wars have been waged around this question of the "one answer," which seems to be a Procrustean bed. Our students are individuals and while some approaches are fairly universal, I must acknowledge the complex nature of reading, the power of literacy, and the importance of motivation and engagement along with word-level strategies that can help students make their way through texts. Do we focus on words when we read? Absolutely. Do we need to attend to and appreciate a range of texts? Ditto.

After all, what is the value of learning to read if you never want to actually use your reading skills? See the box below for more about this.

## What Skills Are Used in Reading Comics?

- Attendance to the written word.
- Attendance to verbal/nonverbal direct and indirect characterization.
- Inferences built across panels and grids.
- Inferences built with attention to expressions and movements.
- Understandings of narrative constructions that span images and words.
- Inferences based on design.
- Interpretations of realistic and fantastic worlds.
- Understandings genre and storytelling in the medium

**FIGURE 2.3.** Skills Used in Reading Comics.

## Embracing All the Texts

This book is about comics, but this chapter has demonstrated how an approach to this medium can be used as a linking point to a range of texts, including fiction and informational texts. As I will further demonstrate in section two, there are many ways we can draw on comics in instructional sequences that can allow for reading, writing, composing, and creating—and that can be used to address standards for social change as well as learning objectives.

# Disrupting Story Types
# and Composition Expectations
# with Comics

W hen I was a young comics reader, it was not enough for me to encounter characters I loved in books or films; I had to extend the storyline any way I could. I dressed like my favorite characters and imagined their stories happening around me. I used my toys to construct, refashion, and revisit stories. In addition, I filled notebooks with narratives, allowing characters to mingle and meet new challenges. While I did not metacognitively visit the idea of a mentor text, the authorial decisions that creators made in film and comics led me to make decisions about my creations.

No teacher stood over me and insisted that I create in response to the stories I loved, utilizing characters and elements I enjoyed. This was not an assignment. In fact, some teachers even took issue with my creations, as I probably should have been using my class time to practice work with fractions.

One of the elements I try to make sure I point out to students, from young children to graduate students, is the wide range of techniques and possibilities that are contained in comics. Recently, I led a group of preservice teachers through a reading of *New Kid* by Jerry Craft. My immediate connection, beyond talking about the design of the work and the questions that can be posed with Craft's authoring, was *creating*. Comics allow for hybridizing and merging approaches as readers take in visual- and word-based designs.

In the following example, I use the labeling practice of Sara Varon alongside the visual design of John Patrick Green, inspired by the series *Investigators*. The image below was inspired by First Second's *Science Comics: Sharks*. Figure 3.1 demonstrates my merging of styles as a modeling process with K–5 students to explore science topics.

In this example, I adopted Green's style in the first section of the page and included my own approach in the panels at the bottom. What of a student's individual style or way of creating? What about students who might lack the words they are looking for in an initial draft? And what about students who just want to explore a new way to express themselves? For some students, words present difficulties; I am thinking of students with complex communication needs, but also students who simply are not practiced in composing to a great extent. While neither

**FIGURE 3.1.** Labeled Example Using Varon and Green's styles

Green nor Varon's work necessarily lends itself to a particular critical issue, my implementation of their texts does return to the question: *What counts as reading?* And in this case, what counts as an opportunity for writing for the classroom?

The central focus of writing and creating leads to some sense of meaning-making and communication. In my teaching, I work to expand possibilities for reading and writing, as noted by Horn and Giacobbe (2007). Authors and artists encourage me to reconceptualize what success looks like in the classroom, and I celebrate creative methods of composing. I believe that the story each of my students brings with them is powerful and matters, and I believe that each of my students matters. By embracing communication styles and methods, I work to open doors for a story to be told in a new way—and perhaps for a brand-new story to be shared.

In a recent interview with author/creator Ben Clanton, he noted how comics gave him the opportunity to engage with creating through words and images. Does this mean that my engagement with a student would stop at images? Surely not, but I do not want to ignore the power of what Sadoski and Paivio (2013) would call the *imogens*, or images, simply because I want to focus on the words, or *logogens*. Texts can include both and, what is more, frequently do in our digital age.

In fact, many ideas for writing and creating are embedded in the work of authors and artists. When I teach Aaron Blabey's Bad Guys series, I point out how the text works. Blabey includes "rap sheets," which are one of the most complex parts of the books. They include more low-frequency words than much of the dialogue among characters. The features that authors include can be drawn upon, in the same way that text features and text structures inform our navigation of informational texts. In the following example, I draw upon Blabey's style in order to craft a new character.

The Bad Guys books frequently feature animal characters, drawn from popular stories and reconfigured as would-be heroes for humorous effect. In this example, Panel 2 shows my attempt to draw upon Blabey's work. I will also note that this creating took place in the context of a shared reading of the first book in the Bad Guys series. Blabey's unique style inspires creating, as seen in Figure 3.2.

By exploring styles, I attempted to mingle narrative and informational text in the same way that many content area comics published in the past ten years or so do. The representation of content area knowledge is not a direct adaptation but a creative story-supported composition. The first panel features an introduction to the topic, and I intentionally included a series of "I can" statements as a demonstration for teachers. Blabey's style inspired my choices for Panel 2, while the central image (Panel 3) is another exercise in labeling, sharing facts about the animal that I had to research. This creating can lead to group-based research about topics of interest. Further connecting genres, Panel 4 draws on poetic methods, while I chose to include a text-only approach in both Panels 4 and 5. This way, the same page could show several options for composing.

Using digital methods and hand-drawn responses, children are able to craft their stories and explore topics of interest prior to a whole-class sharing. By taking this open and flexible approach to composing, I was able to merge a range of styles in terms of both illustration techniques and composing methods.

Following up on these ideas about literacy opportunities and approaches to composing, I explore particular avenues of critical inquiry in section two. In each chapter, please note how this critical inquiry is supported by books that I would readily recommend for classroom and school libraries.

As an added feature to close this chapter, I have included the words of a comics creator gathered through an interview. Sara Varon's wordless work

**FIGURE 3.2.** Author-Created Visual/Informational Text Response, Drawing on the Style of Bad Guys

repositions the power of the image and consideration of the word as a primary method of storytelling. Students in my classes have marveled at her wordless graphic novel, *Robot Dreams,* for many years now.

Varon was kind enough to talk with me in June 2022 and shared a glimpse of her work for this book in Figure 3.3.

**FIGURE 3.3.** Image Courtesy of Sara Varon

## An Interview with Sara Varon

*Why are wordless comics important?*

**Sara Varon:** Comics with no words are a great place to start because words just take precedence over pictures in our culture. So, you really could read the words without looking at the pictures. If there are no words, you really have to look at the pictures, and I feel like that's a good strategy for people who are new to comics.

*Please tell us about your creative process.*

**Sara Varon:** It changes. It takes me so long to do a book that it changes from book to book. With early books, I would think about what I wanted to draw. I thought about what feelings I wanted to leave the reader with, and so for *Bake Sale* and *Robot Dreams*, I wanted to explore the idea that things don't always work out the way you want and how you make the best of that. I think that's probably much more common for most people. My style changes and my skills change from book to book. Now, I'm working on a mystery, which is really different. With the early books, I didn't know how they were going to end, but for the mystery, you have to plan it all out. It's not as stream-of-consciousness, and there aren't as many surprises in making a mystery. I didn't know how *Robot Dreams* was going to end at all and the same with *Bake Sale*.

*What do graphic novels let storytellers do that's different from prose?*

**Sara Varon**: I really love character design, and there is no character design in a novel except what the reader brings to it. There is so much you can show. I can describe how characters look. I made a character sheet for my latest graphic novel. Many times, my characters are based on friends' pets. You can show a personality in the way a character looks. Different people take in means of communication differently. So, for some people it would be so much easier to get somebody's personality across by showing it. I am not great with words, which is why *Robot Dreams* started out as a wordless comic. That's a much easier way for me to communicate—visually rather than verbally. I think my books are about what's going on around me. I hope older and younger readers can both tap in. There's something for everybody, regardless of your reference point.

*What do you see as the place for graphic novels for readers?*

**Sara Varon**: Everybody has different strengths and different ways that they take in information. I just saw a note about Mike Cavallaro's book about free speech, which is for high school students and adults. For some people, taking in information that way is easier and more enjoyable. You want to get a message across and some people might need a book about politics that is only words.

*What is the message you want to send through your books?*

**Sara Varon**: I had a teacher in my graduate illustration program who said that people have a theme that they stick with their whole lives. I don't know if creators pick it, or if it just is what it is. For some reason, mine seems to be friendship. Whatever I make seems to be about characters who are friends. In a number of my books, there's a message of helping someone do the right thing. I would like to think that most people who hurt other people are not doing it on purpose. I would like to think that most people are good. When people make hurtful decisions, I like to think they wouldn't make those choices if they knew how other people felt about it, and that they can be made aware.

# II

# Carefully Constructed Text Windows Using Graphic Novels

# Antibias and Addressing
# Bullying in Visual Works

As I noted in the introduction, each of the following chapters will include anchor standards from *Learning for Justice* to serve as a guiding framework for linking critical issues and topics with the books that I foreground. Ideas in this chapter, for me, most clearly connect with these two standards:

- *Learning for Justice — Diversity Anchor Standard 9. Students will respond to diversity by building empathy, respect, understanding and connection.*
- *Learning for Justice — Justice Anchor Standard 11. Students will recognize stereotypes and relate to people as individuals rather than representatives of groups.*

In this chapter, I explore The Bad Guys series by Aaron Blabey not only in the way that the text is composed, which I have just explored, but also related to the questions that Blabey takes up. These questions include possibilities for fruitful discussion around disrupting traditional expectations of characters through anti-bullying and antibias education. Kuh et al. (2016) defined antibias education as, "a way of teaching that supports children and their families as they develop a sense of identity in a diverse society" (p. 58). These researchers draw on the Eliot-Pearson Children's School's framework for antibias education, which includes entry points for conversation as well as working with feelings, thoughts, responses, and sharing (Kuh et al., 2016, p. 59). The work calls upon teachers to give close consideration to interactions, curriculum, and topics, among other aspects of classroom experience. A sense of welcome is an essential ingredient in my recipe for a healthy classroom and working environment.

## Exploration of Bad Guys Series

While black-and-white film was not always a popular choice in my classroom, Blabey's monochromatic scheme meets humor and creativity to create an engaging style. The books are composed in a black-and-white style, with large images and easy-to-read faces, and the titular group of "Bad Guys" include Mr. Wolf, Mr. Snake, Mr. Shark, and Mr. Piranha. I have been intrigued by the positive response the book has received when I have used it in classrooms, and note the reactions of students, from third grade to high school, who encounter the book. I have chosen it first as it is often the favorite text that teachers share work on from the text ladders I help them construct.

*The Bad Guys* (the first book in the series) is one of the rare titles that I heard about first from children, as the books were recommended to me from student interns working in the field with third graders in 2018. The series has continued to gain traction and is one of the few books from 2018 that I continue to hear rave reviews about. The simple style, use of humor, and imaginative storytelling that Blabey employs are aspects that appeal to readers. As mentioned earlier, there are lengthier sections where information about the Bad Guys is presented in the form of rap sheets. These are the parts of the text that are especially salient for older readers to build further vocabulary around, but these are also the parts that might lead to more pre-teaching opportunities for building background knowledge.

In direct address, Mr. Wolf greets the reader and explains the plot in the first few pages, as he lays out a storyline that subverts what readers might expect from characters in stories. The approach is an example of breaking the fourth wall and the audience being welcomed in as part of the evolving story. This connection between the character and reader allows for humor but is also relational.

*The Bad Guys* can be used to help readers think about character attributes in close ways, and the books have the fun and appealing appearance of a children's comic combined with the potential for posing deeper questions. The first book was adapted into a 2022 film, opening up possibilities for working with students across media.

The use of animal characters and popular literary figures is, in itself, a stylistic and narrative move that allows for flexible storytelling and further discussion, including comparisons to more long-held representations of characters. Our next step in a lesson looking at these classical tropes would be to begin to have conversations about the expectations and first impressions readers bring to social situations involving people in the world. How do the author and the artist help us see these traditional characters in new ways? What surprises us about them? How do we relate to them?

While *The Bad Guys* succeeds in an authentic approach to critical issues, some stories that simplify the presence of biases in relationships, as well as bullying, should be examined carefully. What's more, an overly didactic approach to critical questions can sometimes have a less-engaging effect for readers. Many authors and artists I talk with avoid the didactic, preferring to trust the reader to draw conclusions. This is the case with *Bad Guys* stories, as Blabey never jumps into the narrative to provide metacommentary about the ironies he is including.

# Classroom Application Ideas

The approach I share here builds on antibias education, according to the ideas outlined by Vasquez et al. (2019), which includes, "Listening to students' concerns or their responses to picture books enables teachers to know how they are reading and problematizing their worlds" (n.p.). When it comes to criticality, I return to Vasquez et al. (2019) frequently throughout these chapters. This consideration links well with the close noticing we as educators expect of ourselves and that we encourage our students to develop for social interactions, including the need for welcoming and inclusive environments, and the close reading of texts as critical educators and consumers. Ironically, adults can learn and relearn these messages and benefit from them, as we work to create environments people want to be part of and as we make critical decisions about the agents of change we want to be in the world around us. I strongly advocate for teachers to be leaders in this work, which means that our conversations, actions, and decisions are living models that extend from the texts we use—not as perfect beings, but as living mentor texts in progress who can share our thinking with students as we negotiate the complex questions of life (see the box below).

## Questions to Apply to Comics/ Multimodal Texts

1. How are characters represented in what I am reading?
2. Who is left out of the story?
3. Who has the power and agency?
4. How is power and agency presented visually?
5. Which characters are given the aspects of strength (e.g., saving other characters)?
6. Who is doing the writing?
7. Who is doing the drawing and/or designing?
8. What message am I receiving from this work?

**FIGURE 4.1.** Sample Questions for Building Critical Awareness

Series books hold a special possibility for readers. There is more ground to cover, and I have practiced asking students to think about the visual design of characters, as well as talking about (and sometimes in the voice of) what characters might sound like, an approach I have adapted from the "Talk Like a Character" idea in Opitz and Rasinski's (2008) work. As a reminder, it can be helpful to expose students to potentially difficult vocabulary words (e.g., piranha, as well as the words found within the character rap sheets) by encouraging multiple and meaningful exposures to these words. What might seem like a relatively simple text can include both opportunities for rich discussion and developed vocabulary learning as the teacher leads students.

Finally, I always seek writing opportunities for students. While the rap sheets form a natural step, I keep in mind that it is important to be sensitive to children who may have family members who are incarcerated. A possible accommodation for this could be presenting these writing/drawing exercises as "character fact sheets" or "character descriptions." Yet I do not want to abridge the power of the book for leading to meaningful conversations. It is ultimately the professional decision of the teacher, following the lead of the particular student, as to whether this aspect of the book becomes a space for processing, writing, and discussion.

The book *Wish* by Barbara O'Connor, for example, also contains a story of an incarcerated parent. I have been amazed to see preservice teachers work with children in tutoring sessions, allowing stories of dealing with this reality to be shared. I note all credit to O'Connor as the author who made this decision and my students who have been brave enough to be open to these discussions. Sometimes the best work I do is led by the students, and sometimes they lead learning in other directions, expressing interests and needs in terms of both emotional processes and reading skills to develop.

## Steps for Further Work
## (Including Additional Resources/Book Titles)

In addition to the titles that I have included in this chapter, I note possibilities in the verse novel *Rhyme Schemer* by K. A. Holt for thinking about bullying and antibias education. While not a graphic novel, *Rhyme Schemer* still works in intriguing ways as Holt presents the reader with opportunities for a close look at a character who is both a bully and bullied. Holt achieves what I thought was impossible—namely, that I would grow to love a bully across the space of a book. The main character in the story is a poet, but one who would not take up the mantle immediately, choosing to rip the pages out of classic texts and reconstitute them as his own verse-infused creations, a humorous and creative visual feature of the book. I have used the book in a course that is focused on the reader who is striving and/or reluctant.

I have also had middle school students readily engage with Rodman Philbrick's *Freak the Mighty* and love the graphic novel work of Damian Alexander (2021) in *Other Boys*. Alexander shares a personal story of growing up as a member of the LGBTQ+ community, experiencing bullying and microaggressions from both fellow students and adults. For further graphic novel recommendations, readers can check out *My Own World* by Mike Holmes, a book that fictionally (and visually) explores a young boy's experiences with bullying and trauma and his escape into a fantasy world as a way of dealing with real life (see the box below).

## Questions for Considering Bias in the Classroom

1. In what ways does bias appear in my life?

2. What are the stories that I silence or that challenge me in my thinking?

3. In what ways do I craft a learning environment where conversations about bias and anti-bullying education can occur?

4. What is the role of my school leadership in supporting a positive environment?

5. How can texts lead me to important and critical conversations with my students?

6. How can I think about welcoming ways to confront bias using reading experiences?

**FIGURE 4.2.** Further Questions for Critical Awareness.

# Stories of Self
# in Autobiographical
# and Biographical Graphic Novels

- *Learning for Justice—Identity Anchor Standard 2. Students will develop language and historical and cultural knowledge that affirm and accurately describe their membership in multiple identity groups.*

As is the case with the first text I introduced, *When Stars Are Scattered* by Victoria Jamieson and Omar Mohamed, graphic novels can serve as textual spaces for sharing stories that are true, resonant, and personal. While some people assume that comics are only about superheroes, this is simply not the case.

In this chapter, I explore the growing number of mainstream autobiographical graphic novels, giving attention to the origin of the comic book memoir and the variety of texts that are increasingly available. The graphic novel medium is growing by leaps and bounds, and it is encouraging to see such a wide variety of voices centered in comics—while also noting that there are still not nearly enough and that there are more stories to be told. A quick glimpse at a classroom shelf can provide insight into missing pieces of experience, as well as those that are seen over and over again.

As critical educators, we can take notice of the stories and experiences our libraries are short on, and we can consider many pathways for telling stories through multimodal texts like graphic novels (and other kinds of texts, too). I would be remiss if I did not mention the ways some groups have used book bans to try to silence access to lived experiences and the feelings of hurt and harm that silencing these voices can create for students who would otherwise see themselves represented in a text (Dallacqua, 2022). I paraphrase author/artist Damian Alexander's wisdom from a virtual author visit: We are all living stories that have yet to be fully told. Alexander, as mentioned in the last chapter, is the creative voice behind the 2021 book *Other Boys*, a graphic novel memoir that explores LGBTQ+ experiences.

Graphic novels contain the work in both the visual and the verbal, allowing for representations of lived experiences across both ways of sharing ideas. As Chute (2008) wrote, "Comics might be defined as a hybrid word-and-image form in which two narrative tracks, one verbal and one visual, register temporality spatially" (p. 452). By using comics, writers have the opportunity to share time in both forms, and readers can shape meaning from the interaction of both the pictorial and word-based meaning-making that is contained on comics pages. The picture book/graphic novel *My Pencil and Me* by Sara Varon (2020) can be a mentor text for young creators. This book draws upon graphic novel grammar and features in the same way that Mo Willems's Elephant and Piggie series does, and features the author as a character in the story, faced with the challenge of authoring an original work. Is it a children's picture book? Is it a comic? In truth, Varon's book includes features of both in a hybrid form. Books that defy easy categorization hold a special place in my heart and practice.

There is much to unpack as more and more authors tell their stories in this merged format that comics allow for, expanding well beyond the superhero narratives that punctuate so many popular comics. Charles Hatfield has written about the prevalence of the superhero story in the comics format, but examples of comics reaching back to the 1940s and 1950s expand well beyond this subgenre of science fiction. EC Comics, for example, featured comics that took place in settings much like westerns and included stories that could be considered part of the mystery and crime genre, as well as horror comics. These latter examples, in particular, drew the ire of concerned parents and stakeholders who questioned the use of violent and sexualized stories in a medium that was readily consumed by young readers.

Autobiographical comics themselves have a history located in underground and adult-oriented graphic novel readership, including *Fun Home* by Alison Bechdel, a text I will explore in more detail in a later chapter. Tom Hart explores the methods Bechdel used to compose *Fun Home,* including family photographs for representational drawings in his book *The Art of the Graphic Memoir: Tell Your Story, Change Your Life*. Students can find new ways to tell their stories, maybe even using drawings when they do not yet have language for their experiences, through comics and hybrid forms. I include a number of questions for exploring memoir comics in the box below.

## Topics for Crafting Memoir Comics

1. How can I represent the languages I speak at home and at school?

2. What does my life look like on the page?

3. What experiences can be rendered more completely using images?

4. What do my feelings look like in pictures?

5. What is the visual/comics map of my journey (so far)?

6. What would I change about myself, and how could whatever I change become a strength or power in my story?

7. What family artifacts/photographs can I use to help me share my life?

**FIGURE 5.1.** Questions to Consider When Crafting Comics Memoir

Henry Jenkins has noted how memory and nostalgia work in collecting culture related to comics in his book *Comics and Stuff*, and he has explored the concept of branding elsewhere. Digital culture has opened up many additional possibilities for linking back to pre-internet aspects of popular culture, reaching a base of fandom from youth to all stages of adulthood (Geraghty, 2018). Even in the world of film, nostalgia continues to be a force that leads storytelling, and the same is true for the new iteration of old toys that make their way back to stores as families build intergenerational connections around some of the characters and stories they have come to love.

As scholars have noted, the comics medium is one of a range of visual formats that allow for informational composing (Dallacqua & Peralta, 2019; Duncan et al., 2013). From science to history to additional topics, comics writers and artists use the medium for many purposes. Additionally, comics serve as a space for exploring stories of self (Connors, 2015; Miller, 2014; Whitlock, 2006).

## Brief Statement on the Relevance of One Chosen Text/Author

In this chapter, I suggest expanding beyond *When Stars Are Scattered* to explore how authors and artists tell their stories in visual memoirs. *Stars* is memoir-driven, and I have fond memories of the author, Omar Mohamed, visiting one of my graduate classes via Zoom. Omar brought with him a sense of kindness, a willingness to engage even though it was late in the night where he was, and a passion for the story he has to share. This book is, once more, the collaboration of Omar's story and memories and the visual depictions of memory from Victoria Jamieson in much the same way that Charise Harper collaborated with artist Rory Lucey to tell part of her childhood story in the 2021 graphic novel *Bad Sister*.

The chosen text to highlight is *Stargazing* by Jen Wang, a book that explores the intersection of Asian American experiences alongside experiences of grief and mental/physical health. While the book is not a strict memoir, it is inspired by experiences that the author/artist Jen Wang shares at the end of the book. Events based in truth can be a powerful example for young readers, both for development of story and engagement in graphic novels (see also Sarah Winifred Searle's 2022 graphic novel *The Greatest Thing*).

# Exploration of Stargazing

*Stargazing* includes both fictionalized storytelling and memory in a way that can encourage creative exploration and storytelling among children. It also includes a focus on intersections of experience based on culture and gender that children might find inviting and relatable. Wang plays with the graphic novel format with floating characters and images that work outside of a traditional comics structure and includes representations of languages through the environment (a topic that I will explore in more detail in Chapter 11).

*Stargazing* is based on real-life experiences, which the author/artist explores in an afterword—complete with photographs. Seeing this use of photography alongside writing, in combination with the artistic work in the story, can serve as a multilayered mentor text all within one book. Teachers can take steps into photographic and visual memoirs as ways for students to think about sharing their own stories.

As with other examples I have included, Wang begins the book wordlessly and leaves the reader to make inferences in the first four pages as they are introduced to Christine, the main character. I love it when an artist/author begins wordlessly because this choice invites the reader to consider the images first and get in the mindset of noting all that the page contains. Through Christine's eyes, the reader meets Moon, a secondary character who is introduced as someone rumored to beat people up. The book can lead to many ideas for discussing the presentation of aspects of Chinese American culture, as well as Buddhism. Additionally, elements of popular culture like K-pop are introduced in the story.

Through images that are not bound by panels, Wang illustrates the two characters bonding over dance moves and experiencing childhood friendship. This panel-free work continues in key places in the narrative, breaking up the predictable panel structure that is found in many comics, and the wordless panels and pages return, relying on the reader to take a close reading of the expressions characters have on their faces as well as the movements and interactions depicted within the images. Examples of movement from language to language are included via K-pop lyrics (p. 77, bottom).

Moon has physical challenges to overcome as the narrative unfolds, resulting in both emotional and mental consequences that can be explored with students. This experience is shared through the eyes of Christine, who is making sense of her friend's condition, and Wang revisits these moments for further life-based explanation at the end of the book. While *Stargazing* is fictional, the narrative allows the author/artist to reflect on experiences in a way that can serve as a mentor text for young readers. This book invites questions of how to share stories that allow for processing life while also establishing our boundaries as storytellers in how much we want to disclose and how much we want to explore through make-believe.

Normalizing growth, challenges, and the permission to be human is an aspect of my classroom I hope to practice well, and I hope that my approach inspires my students to lead and learn as our classes work in the community to improve the systems at work around us. From this vantage, I began my classes at the university level by reading a commonly drafted department statement on inclusivity, which I was active in shaping. At the conclusion of this statement, I invite students to talk with me at any point about the environment that I hope to welcome along with them.

Of course, *Stargazing* does not offer an all-in-one stop, but what it offers is worth visiting. The target audience for the book is upper elementary and middle grades; nevertheless, the flexible nature of the images and text means that this book can be accessible to a wide range of readers. Some maturity is required to empathize with Moon, who experiences visions. This element of the story is also part of its strength, acting as a mental/physical health underpinning that can open up additional conversations.

To build upon discussion, students can explore the layers of experience presented in the facto-fiction graphic novel, including the intersections of gender and Asian American culture, as well as the mental health challenges that the characters face. The text is one that demonstrates a growing awareness of the importance of friendship and the ways friendship can be challenged and ultimately mature as a result of difficulties in life.

As hinted at the end of the book, *Stargazing* is an example of self-disclosure and personal exploration on the part of the author/artist. Stories allow the author to process and revisit experiences from the distance of the printed page or etched illustration, allowing fiction to fill in the gaps where needed. As I explore often with authors and creators on my podcast, sharing narratives is also a way for connections to happen with readers so that both author/primary voice and audience knows they are not alone.

## What to Look For

While *Stargazing* serves as a strong and authentic example, I suggest care in sharing nonfiction/memoir-oriented texts from cultural outsiders or onlookers who are depicting someone else's story. This lack of firsthand experience can undermine an otherwise well-designed text, leading to a surface-level narrative that centers around cultural or social assumptions. I find myself doing additional work to find out who authors are, what history they have within the context of a given topic, and what they bring to the story with them. This insider's perspective speaks to the authentic experience of an author while I also honor creativity in exploring stories from alternative perspectives. Taking a close look at who creators are does take some additional time and research, but information about the voices and lives behind the book is generally readily available on publisher and author websites. I hesitate to take a biography study approach in the classroom every time my students read a book, but it can be helpful to point out details about the author in the moment and in context while reading.

I strive to be authentic about my limitations as a white male, and there are quite simply stories for which I am not the primary voice. Helpfully, there are authors and artists whose amazing and impactful work I can take with me each time I step in front of a class to engage with learners, whether the audience is K–12 or beyond.

As a literacy educator, I believe stories should be honored, told, and retold. A function of honoring a story is recognizing the voice that is sharing the story and noting that the voice carries weight when there is authenticity behind it. Teachers can ask students to do some of this looking too, inviting them to ask why a source is well positioned to speak to a topic and, if writing from another perspective, where viewpoints and details might differ.

## Classroom Application Ideas

While state standards and curricular demands may prioritize words, there is a power to be found in embracing visual forms for children in order to share their stories. Seeing multiple stories told in this medium can serve as a mentor text experience, showing young writers tools they might use to engage in craft.

Listening to and inviting the stories that others/those who are othered might offer us is courageous and human work. Children bring the issues of life with them, reflected in the classroom, and texts can be connection points. Some of the issues and questions that children explore can be windows into the wider questions of society and even of life. Readers must be in a place to listen to and respect one another in order to authentically engage in these kinds of processes, and we must know that the stories others share are ultimately not about us. One of the tenets of antibias education is supporting and affirming students who may be the object of biases.

Teachers might consider a step-by-step journaling process for young writers, including drawings and photographs, as well as artifacts drawn from home. It might be the case that children will want to share their stories with us; on the other hand, there might be some elements of their personal stories that children will want to keep in the respected boundaries of their own writing spaces. I embrace both approaches, and I suggest care, thoughtfulness, and attention when asking students to share about themselves in class. Our stories are, after all, part of our power, and it is our decision to share them in the way that feels best to us.

Writing is one avenue for students to share their thoughts, experiences, and feelings, and to communicate the memories that are most important to them. The same is true for adults; moreover, writing is a way of hearing and learning about all of the voices gathered in a classroom at the same time and to check in with where students are. Children live complicated lives and may choose to share about themselves in ways that challenge us. Sometimes writing or drawing may be the only way we get to know some students.

A step-by-step process for this memoir and memory-driven work might include the following:

**Step 1: Stop and jot/curate and craft important memories.** Stems might include: What stands out as a shaping event? What is an important happening in your life so far? What is the story of one good day? What is a story that you want to share with the world?

Students might be encouraged to bring in family photographs or artifacts from home to serve as writing inspirations and/or representations to use in their drawings. Memories take time, so beginning with this part of the process can be helpful.

**Step 2: Mentor text methods**. This part of the process can include looking at multiple examples of memoir/memory-based comics, as well as artwork and creations from the teacher-as-mentor.

Seeing the way that authors, artists, and the teacher have gone about engaging in this work before is a roadmap forward.

**Step 3: Brainstorming.** This can be done with questions, including how many panels are needed, what parts of a personal story to include, and how much detail students are comfortable sharing. Setting these boundaries is important human work, and teachers might suggest that students list what happened in a sequence of written steps before adapting their thinking to comics form. It is also practice in our classrooms to disclose to students up front that they do not have to share details they are not comfortable with anyone else knowing; the space of a private page is still a place of powerful authorship.

Students read aloud sections of their own writing only when they want to, and they share with us only what they wish. While this approach might reframe the power dynamic of turning papers in for a grade, I believe it makes writing a comfortable activity and process for my students.

**Step 4: Writing and sharing.** With this work done and evolving in the class-room, which can be a workshop-like space, I suggest giving students the space and time to create personal notebooks. They can then have an author's chair experience to share their work—or not, depending on how comfortable they are.

*Digital work:* As an additional idea for composing memoirs, I again point to using photographs in digital form to tell photo-comics, or comics-like stories told using real objects and images of living people that are part of the author/artist's life. Photos often form a part of an artifact-based practice in linking together elements of stories, and they can often be seen at the conclusion of graphic novel memoirs as author/artists inform the reader of the real-life under-pinnings behind the story.

Randall and Mercurio (2015) wrote about classrooms as places where objects and memories ("stuff," as the title of their article suggests) can be collected and celebrated. They drew upon the work of Pahl and Rowsell (2011), authors of *Artifactual Literacies: Every Object Tells a Story* (2019). From a critical perspective, classrooms can be places where voices can be heard through both the literature that children consume and the literature that they create. Children should not be limited in the ways they can tell stories. I have also had some students who prefer to compose primarily in written words, and this is a welcome approach as well.

Classrooms are, ideally, studio-like spaces where teachers can guide children in inquiry, drawing on memory and experience, exploring the world, and dis-covering the voices of a range of people, some of whom have historically been silenced or sidelined. Classrooms can be artistic places where students can cel-ebrate what they know, extend into places where they are less familiar, and use a variety of tools for responding as well as a variety of languages.

Photos themselves can form the impetus, as well as the mode, of creation. The image in Figure 5.2 was crafted as a mentor text for students in a summer literacy clinic, and it demonstrates the fusion of comics elements with real-life images of the author's pets. Such instances of home form the basis of the experi-ences that students draw on, and teachers can learn a great deal from the arti-facts that children share, including elements of culture.

These images are from my own home, and I used digital text and edit-ing to support dialogue and descriptions, uniting written words with the images. I recommend creating mentor texts in any writing engagement, as well as writing with children, composing models that they can use when they practice (Gallagher, 2014). I further recommend using student work as additional mentor texts for inspiring further creations. Comics can allow stories to be read and seen, and writers should be exposed to examples when working.

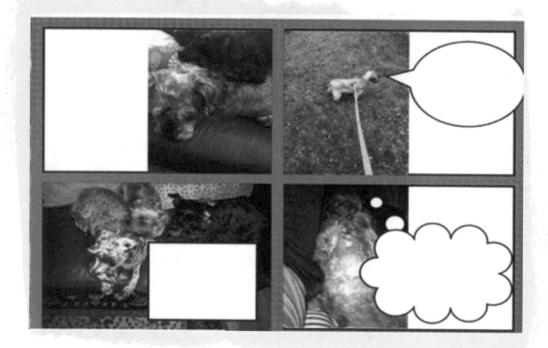

**FIGURE 5.2.** An Example of a Photo-Comic

## Steps for Further Work
## (Including Additional Resources/Book Titles)

As hinted early in this chapter, memoirs in comics format have been around for a while, and this is a growing subgenre of the medium. Additional texts to highlight include *Messy Roots: A Graphic Memoir of a Wuhanese American* by Laura Gao, *Sylvie* by Sylvie Kantorovitz, and *Becoming RBG* by Debbie Levy and Whitney Gardner. Each of these books offers a unique vision of making, from the shifts in time and place in Goa's work with comics/graphic novels to a visual/verbal memoir of growing up by Kantorovitz to a nonfiction look at another person's life by Levy and Gardner.

*Becoming RBG* has the additional benefit of working as a clear example of researched creation, as the author and artist share their references at the end of the book. Examining the materials authors include in the last pages can serve as its own source of inspiration.

Additional examples include Vera Brosgol (2018) in *Be Prepared* and Lucy Knisley (2020) in *Stepping Stones*. These titles also use images and true stories to inspire their content. As with *Stargazing*, the reader may be surprised to find the links to inspiration at the end of the book. Author/artist Tyler Page (2022) even included childhood artwork in the back of his graphic novel exploration of growing up with ADHD, *Button Pusher*.

A number of texts are available for older/high school and young adult readers as well, featuring stories from a wide range of communities, including *Parenthesis* by Élodie Durand (2021) and *The Best We Could Do: An Illustrated Memoir* by Thi Bui (2018). In each of these books, storytelling takes on the fashion of memories in the unique style of the creator. In the case of *Parenthesis*, the inner, subjective experiences of a person/character with a brain tumor are visually depicted. Writers in our classrooms deserve a range of tools with which to demonstrate what they are accomplished at, what they are processing, and what they have yet to grow in.

It is one benefit to encounter a story with all of the beauty and possibility that fantasy and fiction can afford. It is quite another to encounter the story of someone who has been where the reader is or who has an experience that can serve as a mirror for readers to see themselves in (Sims Bishop, 1990). Books hold this power in helping us know that we are not alone and that our stories resonate with people across place and across time. This is the quiet conversation between author/artist and reader.

Teachers might consider the following questions as they engage with memoir graphic novels:

1. What stories are most centralized in my curriculum?
2. Whose voices are left out in my classroom?
3. What tools do my students need to share their story?
4. In what ways can I centralize student voices as a weekly or daily part of writing instruction?
5. In what ways can I centralize composing, even briefly, in response to readings in my class?
6. How do images and digital tools open up possibilities for storytelling for my students?

As a final section in this chapter, I include words from author and artist Chad Sell, whose anthology comics work *The Cardboard Kingdom* features a host of stories that draw upon superhero characters to weave narratives in familiar settings. I recommend this book series, as well as the *Doodleville* books that Sell has crafted, for additional thinking about how comics can be used to show types of storytelling. Both of these titles are entries in ongoing series and opportunities to hook readers. You can see an example of this work provided by Sell in Figure 5.3 on the following page.

**FIGURE 5.3.** Image Courtesy of Chad Sell

## Words from Creator Chad Sell

*What's your author origin story?*

**Chad Sell**: I grew up reading superhero comics. I grew up before the manga boom in the United States, so my imagination was shaped by early '90s superhero comics, video games, and science fiction and fantasy. I would look at my favorite comics and draw my favorite characters in poses. I started doing my own comics in high school and branched out into different genres of comics. I was influenced by indie creators of that time, so I started doing webcomics. In college, I started doing a weekly newspaper comic strip. After college, I tried to tackle full-length graphic novels. I was a little ambitious and thought I would immediately be a published author and had an unrealistic idea of what making books was like. It was a long, rocky road to *The Cardboard Kingdom* in 2018. I was making a living with my art before that, through freelance illustrations and selling books at comics conventions.

*So, superhero comics were a draw for you?*

**Chad Sell:** There's something about the outsized heroics, like colorful costumes. A lot of my favorite comics also had big feelings, too. A lot of people talk about classic *X-Men* stories as being a kind of long soap opera story, with all of these characters exploring identity, having interpersonal conflicts, and trying to reach their full potential. I deeply relate to all of that.

The Cardboard Kingdom *is kind of an anthology, right?*
**Chad Sell:** That came about because I had tried multiple times to sell books to publishers. I had worked on a bunch of different adults' and kids' projects. I am very self-critical, and I think that helps me improve, but it can be difficult when you are working on a longer project. I wasn't sure at that point if I was able to do a book by myself, so I started thinking about collaboration. I did "The Sorceress Next Door" with my friend Jay Fuller and had worked on it as a minicomic to sell at conventions, and we really liked the story. I had this idea of a whole book that could feature kids in a neighborhood, following their stories. I wasn't sure who those kids would be. I started seeing a lot of crowdfunding, and I thought about a similar approach. I used the web to find writers in search of an artist and who might be interested in the concept. I had a website for a few months for writers to send story ideas in, and that's how I found the ten authors I worked on the book with.

*How do you see the book in literacy instruction?*
**Chad Sell:** I hope that *The Cardboard Kingdom*, because of its anthology nature, has flexibility. So, if a teacher wants to excerpt a chapter, they can use it and have a conversation about it. Maybe have them broken up and have different groups talk about different chapters. It's so cool to see different projects that come from classrooms when they use the book. I saw one recently that used the map in the book, and the students created cardboard dioramas. It was so cool to see my drawing fleshed out with swings for stuffed animals. I was so impressed, and it's amazing and magical to see a student be so creative.

# Gender Representation in Graphic Novels

- *Learning for Justice—Identity Anchor Standard 5. Students will recognize traits of the dominant culture, their home culture, and other cultures and understand how they negotiate their own identity in multiple spaces.*
- *Learning for Justice—Justice Anchor Standard 11. Students will recognize stereotypes and relate to people as individuals rather than representatives of groups.*

## Considering the Role of Gender in Comics

The presentation of female characters and characters who present as female in comics has a complicated history, as noted by scholars like Hilary Chute and Carolyn Cocca. This set of complications includes the notion of oversexualized depictions and objectified depictions of women as the focal point of an objective viewpoint, as well as the historically minoritized/diminished role that women comics creators have played, particularly in mainstream publications. I begin by noting, once more, that my identity/identities as a white cisgender male entails additional considerations, including the help of critical friends, to assist me in my thinking about how to best and most respectfully approach authentic representations of experiences that I do not share.

Again, thinking of Alison Bechdel, whom I mentioned in the last chapter, I note the presence of female creators in the comics field is often relegated to underground comix. The term *comix* denotes a movement of creators whose work stood in contrast to the mass-produced texts of their time, beginning in 1968 with the publication of *Zap Comix* (Rosenkranz, 2002). I also point to writers and creators like Nancy Collins, Barbara Kaalberg, June Brigman, G. Willow Wilson, and Gail Simone, whose work has featured characters in the popular mainstream, all of whom have worked in an industry that has been overwhelmingly dominated by male creators and editors.

As I noted earlier, Henry Jenkins suggested that the historically assumed audience of comics is adolescent males. I hope this exploration of the range of graphic novels and comics that are available for readers to enjoy, both for personal reading and classroom instruction, serves as pushback on both the assumed age and gender of comics' readership. I also note once more that a large number of comics creators, from a historical perspective, have been male. In an analysis of newspaper comics, only eleven percent of creators (authors or artists) were women (Glascock & Preston-Schreck, 2004).

The growing number of female and nonbinary voices in the medium suggests that comics are for everyone and that making comics is not a gendered practice nor is reading them relegated to only an objectifying and limited male view. As Moeller (2011) has pointed out, comics and graphic novels belong to other strands of culture and are not simply books for young male readers.

In this chapter, I draw attention to the work of artists/authors like Tillie Walden, Noelle Stevenson, Mollie Knox Ostertag, and Raina Telgemeier for creating and sharing texts that challenge gender stereotypes in graphic novel form while also providing space for challenging assumptions and biases about gender in society. I also recommend the work of Liana Kangas, Lilah Sturges, Marley Zarcone, and Zoe Thorogood.

Returning to *When Stars Are Scattered* as a central linking text, I draw attention to how women are depicted as both agents of change in the book as well as the ways that Omar Mohamed and Victoria Jamieson show that opportunities for women have been stifled—an act of artistic activism, or artivism, that serves as a textual point for societal change.

As part of this chapter, I include lessons that teachers can use to engage the topic of gender stereotyping and bias, and I discuss the importance of a variety of representations in graphic novels for children and adolescents. From linking back to *Stars*, I next highlight *Nightlights* by Lorena Alvarez as an exemplary text, one with a beauty and style all its own.


## Looking at *Nightlights*

*Nightlights* by Lorena Alvarez is a relatively short graphic novel that includes a female central character. When it comes to length, I am less concerned about the number of pages and more concerned about the rich opportunities for rereading that are afforded by comics. I myself have read a 22-page comic multiple times while only attending to a 400-page novel one time. *Nightlights* is an example of Künstlerroman, a narrative that explores the early formation of an artistic or authorial character. The main character in question, Sandy, spends time getting lost in her creations, drawing with great detail. The reader is first introduced to her as she lies on the floor, filling up notebooks with sketches, as her mother calls her from outside the frame. Like the main character in Holmes's *My Own World,* Sandy has crafted an interior world into which she can escape—with supernatural and intriguing consequences. The comics style vividly draws both reality and the fantasy world in stark contrast to one another.

Upon entering the fantasy world, Sandy soon meets a doppelganger character, Morfie, who might be an actual person in the narrative as a malevolent force or might be a projection of her inner doubts and fears as a young artist trying to come to grips with the world around her. The story is complex yet told in an accessible way. This nuance and lack of direct narrative answer can lead to discussions about Morfie as an imagined or real force, and the symbolism of the book can be further explored.

Alvarez's art is inviting, and it is easy to see how a young person might be swept away by the intricacies of these designs. The character of Morfie can be a bit frightening at times—a presentation that may be a topic of interest to tackle when reading or which might actually work to create appeal for some young readers. In their first experience with the book, one of the graduate students in a 2020 course I taught responded by creating their own mandala-style work. Sandy must discover how she manages Morfie's presence in her life. She is, ultimately, not a character who is rescued but one who discovers a sense of empowerment as she works through questions of her inner life. Sandy arrives at the critical decision to fight back against the darker aspects of this inward journey/supernatural encounter, taking up a sense of agency.

While I enjoy the appeal that some stories bring, there is a continuing tendency to position female characters as needing to be rescued by their male counterparts. Female characters are not mere foils nor are they narrative conveniences for demonstrating the power and dominance of the male characters. Sandy is her own character, working in the real world and in her imagination, and she must find identity and strength in herself to defeat the powers that are aligned against her—powers that are, in essence, representations of her inner challenges.

Alvarez gives us a character who is female and empowered, one who takes ownership of her identity, artistry, and selfhood by the end of the story. These questions of belonging and "fit" in the wider world are relevant for young readers, and teachers can build on them to ask questions and build dialogue as well as more invitations to write and create in response.

## When Books Miss It

For thinking about the presentation of female characters in comics, I can think of no better place to begin than with the Bechdel Test itself. Originally presented by Bechdel in her comics series *Dykes to Watch Out For*, the test has been applied to film but is also useful for consideration in comics reading. (Indeed, comics and film have much in common, though they also work in their own ways.) To pass the Bechdel Test, a movie, comic, or literary work must have (1) at least two women in it (2) who talk to each other (3) about something other than a man. This critical view of a text can help the reader/viewer examine both the presence or absence of female characters as well as their purpose and sense of identity in the overall plot.

These questions are useful in critiquing stories, and next steps can include additional levels of questioning focused on character design and the worlds in which characters exist.

## Critical Questioning: Who Is Drawing?

As is the case with many other intersections of identity and presentations of lived experiences, the graphic features and word-based design of comics hold much value for analysis. To begin with, I ask: Who is doing the drawing? For example, in instances where female characters are portrayed in questionable, subservient, or stereotypical ways, including depictions that are objectifying to women, I ask who the artist is and inquire about their intent. Is the female character the central force of agency, or instead is that character being acted upon? Is the presentation of the character a symbol of their power and intersections of cultural identity, or is it simply a sexualized product?

Cocca (2014) has pointed to variations in the levels of objectifying depictions between the cover-based drawings of women and those found within panels. Notably, when women are a driving creative force, Cocca noted that the presentations of characters are less one-dimensional and objectifying. As is the case with stories told from an authentic, insider experience, this consideration of who is doing the word- and image-based storytelling is worth exploring.

Furthermore, I ask not only who is doing the drawing but also what lived experiences and intersections of identity the artist/author is drawing from. Are depictions set in the frame of subjugation for women? If someone is being rescued, who is doing the rescuing? For what purpose? What are the other ways a narrative might be resolved or a character might grow and change? What is the role of other characters in the narrative in relation to the female/nonbinary character(s)? Who has the primary voice in the narrative and, when speaking, what message are they sending? How does the artistic design and how do the decisions of the artist support or contradict the agency of female/nonbinary characters?

The Bechdel Test can be applied in many ways. Even young readers have begun to be exposed to gender expectations and roles in society, and exploring representations of gender roles and experiences in text can be helpful in building a thoughtful consideration of text. I encourage teachers to lead students in a discussion of questions of characters and settings. See the box below for questions to guide this process.

## Questions of Gender Representation in Comics

1. How are power relationships depicted between characters of different genders?
2. What stereotypical expectations of genders are depicted in character actions and decisions?
3. How many female and nonbinary characters are present in the narrative?
4. What are these characters doing?
5. How are female and nonbinary characters depicted, if present?
6. In what settings are characters of different genders presented?
7. What visual motifs are notable when considering the ways that artists and authors present characters?

**FIGURE 6.1.** Questions to Explore Representation

In this case, the use of a comic/graphic novel depiction can then expand to the use of additional texts in a multimodal text—in fact, I have employed a text set approach like this in classes I have taught. Reading can occur across a range of texts, and these texts can add to one another in a variety of ways. Children can consider how gender is depicted in the comic as well as in prose, film, memes, other social media content, historical and contemporary propaganda, and more. Curating texts includes questions of what decisions authors/artists/auteurs make in changing the dynamics of character relationships, depending on the media being used for storytelling. Even comparing the presentation of a female character in a more recent film to film/television from ten years ago may lead to fruitful discussion (and may be surprising in terms of what culture has considered permissible and entertaining).

In this approach, close reading of characters, including their actions and interactions, is essential, as is close reading of the setting itself. Likewise, in superhero comics, when female/nonbinary characters are presented as members of teams, educators can lead discussions regarding their roles on the team and how they interact as part of the story. Unfortunately, examples from mainstream comics often presented female superhero team members as objects of desire, tokens to battle over, or even the focus of sexual violence. Such limited presentations and one-dimensional treatments of female characters are problematic and only serve to centralize the male characters even more so as the forces of the story that act to rescue or in retaliation.

Laurie Halse Anderson's collaboration with Emily Carroll (2018) on the graphic novel adaptation of Anderson's novel *Speak* is an example of a comics work that takes up the subject of sexual assault in a way that is respectful to the story of the main character. In this book, images and design features are used to convey the fragmented and painful feelings of the main character as she grapples with the abusive experience. The words that Halse Anderson shares form part of this meaning making, while the images work to illustrate emotion.

## Steps for Further Work (Including Additional Resources/Book Titles)

Because of the male-dominated nature of the comics industry, I want to share a range of titles that disrupt the long-held gender imbalance that has been prevalent in the medium. The titles in the table below are worth exploring.

**TABLE 6.1.** A Collection of Texts.

| Book/Author | Brief Synopsis | Key Points |
|---|---|---|
| *Nimona* by Noelle Stevenson | Stevenson shares the story of a young shapeshifting female in a fantasy/science fiction world filled with humor. | The book plays with fantasy tropes in a playful way and presents a female character in a way that does not conform to typical representations. |
| *Marshmallow & Jordan* by Alina Chau | A young girl who is differently abled meets a mystical elephant in a journey to explore her identity as an athlete. | The book, like so many others in our list of recommendations, is beautifully designed. Jordan is a character worth exploring in terms of the intersection of gender, cultural identity, religion, and ableism. |
| *The Prince and the Dressmaker* by Jen Wang | Wang presents the story of a prince who challenges gender stereotypes of fashion, as he prefers to wear dresses. | The book takes on the tropes of the fairy tale genre and travels in new directions so that readers can consider gender identity, expression, and the ways classic stories can reify or challenge stereotypes. |

| | | |
|---|---|---|
| *Zita the Spacegirl* by Ben Hatke | Hatke infuses the narrative with mythical and other-worldly creatures as the main character and hero, Zita, races to save her best friend. | Though written by a male author, *Zita* centers a female character as a strong protagonist in a science-fiction story. The elements of genre work for readers who may connect with fantasy and science fiction. |
| *The Witch Boy* by Mollie Knox Ostertag | Aster is a young warlock whose use of magic and exploration of identity link more closely to witches. | The book works from a fantastic conceit/vantage to explore what it means to be a person who does not conform to gender expectations in society. |
| *As the Crow Flies* by Melanie Gillman | Gillman explores the intersections of identity for a Black queer female character, Charlie, who is spending the summer at a Christian youth camp with mostly White characters. | The book is, at the time of this writing, available in both a printed form and as a freely accessible webcomic. |
| *Noisemakers* (anthology) | A number of creative artists depict stories of 25 female figures from across time who have changed the world. | The book centers female innovators and figures from the pen of female artists/creators. |
| *Brazen* by Pénélope Bagieu | An exploration of notable women in history, written for a slightly older or young adult audience. | The entries are biographical and episodic, pointing to powerful women throughout history, and Bagieu's style is on display in each telling of historical events. |
| *Lumberjanes* by Noelle Stevenson, Shannon Watters, Grace Ellis, and Gus Allen | An assembly of female characters take on a range of fantastical creatures in this ongoing series. | As mentioned, the book is a series and, once readers are hooked, there is a sprawling world to explore, complete with adventure and humor (two elements so often used as selling points in male-focused narratives but clearly appealing to all readers). A range of artistic talents are showcased in the issues, either through cover art or designs in the books themselves. |
| *Auntie Po* by Shing Yin Khor | A retelling of Paul Bunyan through the vision of a Vietnamese American narrative. | The book is a wonderful example of the intersection of culture and gender identity and is essential work of the imagination for considering perspectives and new takes on stories that readers think they know all about. |
| *Smile* by Raina Telgemeier | A graphic novel memoir of losing teeth, navigating relationships, wearing braces, and exploring identity. | Telgemeier's work is a fixture of the contemporary movement in graphic novels, and her books have been instrumental in popularizing the medium and capturing the attention of young (upper elementary, middle grades, and beyond) readers. |
| *Spinning* by Tillie Walden | A graphic novel memoir exploring the author/artist's avocation for ice skating, as well as her youth and experiences coming to understand her sexuality. | Walden is a young and yet incredibly prolific comics creator who has written books in the science-fiction genre as well as contemporary fiction in graphic novel form. |

For final words in this chapter, I turn to artist/authors Hope Larson and Alina Chau.

# An Interview with Hope Larson

*Please tell us about your creative process.*

**Hope Larson:** I'm a cartoonist, which means I both write and draw comics. Sometimes I do the whole thing on a book, and sometimes I partner with a different artist—it depends on the project. Typically, I write a detailed script for the book that includes dialogue, panels per page, and what's happening visually and emotionally in each panel. That gets edited numerous times before the drawing process begins. I've used a mixture of traditional (i.e., drawn on paper) artwork and digital artwork for my books over the years, but I'm finally shifting to fully digital work in the interest of saving time.

*What female creators/characters would you like to celebrate and center for readers who are looking for authentic representations?*

**Hope Larson:** Authentic representations of what? Girls and women? No character is going to embody the exact experience of any individual, but I'm partial to the characters I've written for myself—Meg Murry from *A Wrinkle in Time* and Barbara Gordon from *Batgirl*. I also love all the characters in my own book, *Salt Magic*, which is a book that grapples with the possibilities for a girl and woman in the early twentieth century. Vonceil, the protagonist, is an adolescent girl who's trying to figure out what kind of future she can realize for herself, and the different characters she encounters on her adventures—Greda the salt witch, Dee the sugar witch, and even her hated sister-in-law Amelia—all offer different possibilities.

*How has the comics industry changed for women, and what still needs to change?*

**Hope Larson:** Less than changing for women, I think the industry urgently needs to change for *everyone*. Better pay, less brutal schedules, and benefits are sorely needed across the board, from book publishers to the Big Two [DC Comics and Marvel Comics]. I've watched so many of my friends put their cartooning careers on hold after having kids because there are no support systems in place to help them, and pay is negligible. It stinks, and it's not sustainable unless you're wildly successful, a hustler, financially supported by a partner, or working some kind of day job.

*Please tell us about the agency and development of female characters in your work and how you encourage young creators to engage in empowering storytelling through comics.*

**Hope Larson:** I try to write characters I feel are complex in the ways real girls and women are—and even, like Vonceil, flawed, angry, and at times unlikeable. I think it's important for kids to see characters who aren't wildly virtuous and overly aspirational. It's important for them to see kids like themselves who make mistakes and still get to be the hero.

## An Interview with Alina Chau

*What inspires you to create?*

**Alina Chau:** I get my creative inspiration from my personal life experiences and my surroundings. At least, that's usually how an idea first sparks in my mind before it expands and develops its own life. After the first spark of inspiration, often, the idea would take me to new, unfamiliar territories when I start exploring. That's when I allow myself to go out of my comfort zone and experiment to see what works and what doesn't.

**FIGURE 6.2.** Image Courtesy of Alina Chau

*Marshmallow & Jordan* (see Figure 6.2) is inspired by my Indonesian Chinese family cultural heritage. When I was little, my grandma often told me stories of her life growing up in Indonesia. At home, she loved making us delicious Indonesian cuisine. During special occasions, she would dress in sarongs with intricate designs. When I was a child, I imagined Indonesia as a tropical paradise filled with rich and colorful textures. When I visited as an adult, it felt like home, though I'd never lived there. I always wanted to write a story about this magical place.

*Please tell us about the visual design of Marshmallow & Jordan (it's really quite beautiful).*

**Alina Chau:** Thank you. Ketut, the fictional town in the book, is a caricature of small towns in Bali, Indonesia. The visual design of the book is strongly influenced by Indonesian Balinese art. Prior to making the book, I took a research trip to Bali and took a lot of reference photos. Some of the scenes in the book are actual streets and locations in Bali. Through the illustrations, I hope to transport readers to Indonesia and introduce them to Balinese culture, scent, and cuisine.

*Please tell us about the ways you centered culture in the book.*
**Alina Chau**: Indonesia's dominant religion is Islam. Marshmallow's image is loosely inspired by Hindu mythology: Airavata, a Hindu rain god. To make Marshmallow fit naturally in the story, I chose Bali as the story's backdrop because Hinduism is the dominant religion in Bali. This would also make having an elephant walking around town feel more believable in a country where seeing an elephant around is not uncommon. The book begins with the illustration of Canang Sari, a little basket offering flowers to the gods. This is a ritual unique to Balinese Hinduism, which Balinese practice daily to express their gratitude for the peace given to the world. Throughout the story, there are subtle hints of Marshmallow's true identity. For example, Marshmallow loves stealing the offering flowers. Marshmallow's magic and the storyline are built upon Hinduism's belief in the harmonious relationship between humanity and nature.

# Diverse Abilities Presented in Comics

- *Learning for Justice—Diversity Anchor Standard 9. Students will respond to diversity by building empathy, respect, understanding, and connection.*
- *Learning for Justice—Justice Anchor Standard 11. Students will recognize stereotypes and relate to people as individuals rather than representatives of groups.*

Building classrooms where all students feel welcome and all voices are celebrated, valued, and heard is important, difficult, and delicate work. It is always my goal to encourage equity and access, and our current climate of polarized perspectives and pandemic living only adds to this challenge. The time teachers spend in thoughtful curation of curriculum, as well as in pedagogical reflection, is well worth what Letizia (2020) explored as a textual approach of hope. While diversity might be part of texts related to gender or ethnicity or race, I am also keenly aware of the ways that characters with disabilities or, as I prefer to put it, characters with diverse abilities are not centralized in many comics narratives. Often, the existence of such characters is implied or not considered at all, and characters with diverse abilities have also been included in comics narratives as villains (for example, the character Legion in the Marvel Comics). At other times, characters with diverse abilities are secondary in the narrative.

Additionally, Letizia (2020) has united the graphic novel with a sense of citizenship development in rendering stories of self-expression. Letizia included their own comic book work as part of the exploration of selfhood and identity. Moeller and Irwin (2012) have advocated for the inclusion of books that represent diverse abilities in classroom and school libraries, and Pennell et al. (2018) have explored children's literature with respectful representations of characters with diverse abilities. I have engaged with Pennell and Koppenhaver in work exploring centralized characters with diverse abilities in comics stories—which has been particularly difficult to locate in comics for younger readers.

# Feature Text: *El Deafo* by Cece Bell

While some texts have explored characters with diverse abilities, *El Deafo* serves as an example that has been written and illustrated by a person who is Deaf. This authentic voice once more helps me consider this to be a strong example of exploring critical connections in a particular graphic novel. Some graphic novels (for example, *Metaphase* by Chip Reece) have been authored by parents of children with diverse abilities. The design of the graphic novel holds appeal for showcasing characters with disabilities/diverse abilities as central players in the world. Unfortunately, not many examples exist.

In *El Deafo*, the presentation of the main character/storyteller is accomplished in a fantastical way—that is, as a superpowered animal character. This presentation creates a sense of wonder and fantasy, which makes the book even more appealing to young readers. Moreover, the fantasy animal character can be seen as a figure of innocence relating to the world around them and as a character more universally relatable than one who is rendered with particular details linking to gender or additional intersections of identity. Upon opening the book, the reader is immediately welcomed with colorful panels and a "regular kid" (Bell, 2014, p. 1) with relatable hobbies, interests, and experiences. Bell's own identity as a person with diverse abilities is woven into the narrative, which has an inviting effect. The book is also informational in many ways, as the reader encounters Bell's journey (again, told through fantasy exploration) in exploring hearing devices and various social situations. The ways that words are depicted on the page illustrates the feeling of loss of hearing as it happens for the main character. The visual lettering/typography in the book is a design feature for both inferencing and creating conversations around this experience (see Figure 7.1).

Specifically, the graphic novel illustrates hearing loss both in the panel to-panel story and as words begin to fade from dialogue bubbles, indicating the change on the part of the main character. Through bright yellow narrative boxes, Bell recounts this story for the reader, at times drawing upon blank dialogue bubbles to demonstrate the loss of hearing in the opening pages. The graphic novel presents a story that not all readers can relate to but which readers can experience along with the main character, creating opportunities for young people to develop empathy—both those who have had similar experiences, who can see themselves represented as a normalizing result of the story, as well as those readers who have not experienced hearing loss. Being a person who is deaf is not viewed in the story as something to engage with in a sympathetic way, but rather the narrative is matter of fact and even heroic at times.

# Questions of a Critical Classroom Stance

1. Who are the students in my classroom, and in what ways might their lives intersect with a range of experiences?

2. What are the stories that are not often told, or even known, in my classroom?

3. Are there characters with diverse abilities present in the books I teach?

4. If so, how are these characters presented? Are they agentive or supplemental to the narrative? Are they objects of sympathy or heroic characters in their story?

5. How and when do students in my classroom have the opportunity to express and explore their identities in writing?

6. Who are the heroes that I often highlight in books? How many of them conform to tropes of ableism?

7. What are the possibilities for using books, including graphic novels, that frame diverse abilities in a positive light and as an integral part of the story structure?

**FIGURE 7.1.** Questions for Classroom Stance

Teachers can consider approaching such representations from the vantage of empathy and explore the strengths of characters with diverse abilities as opposed to constructing classroom environments that focus on these responses of sympathy. Often, narratives that center around diverse abilities/disabilities are stories of "overcoming" rather than descriptions of lived experiences that readers can learn from. There is much agency in Bell's fantastic depiction and note the skills of this author/artist as an additional comics superpower that can be highlighted and discussed. Bell includes a note at the end of the book in which she expands on her experiences and shares details about the inspiration behind the story.

# Engaging in the Work

When reading books about experiences to which I cannot directly relate, I position myself as a learner and seek to discover and share stories that empower. While some books feature characters with diverse abilities, it is advisable to avoid texts where such characters are presented as lesser counterparts, diminished sidekick characters, objects of pity, or characters who simply have something to overcome. At times, characters with diverse abilities may exist in a story but only serve a limited role or function, as in service to the main character as a foil or a character of perceived weakness to be rescued, as we have seen with characters who are female. Likewise, students in our classrooms who may share relatable experiences with characters are themselves not the center of study, nor are they to be approached as the assumed primary speaker for an entire group of people. Rather, an invitation to share about experiences through writing and speaking to the classroom as a welcome but not required source of learning and engagement can be maintained through classroom routines and steps focused on norms for reading and composing stories. Such norms might include those in the box to the right. This brief list is hardly exhaustive, and I encourage teachers to collaborate with one another, as well as administrators, students, and families, to think about what norms can foster the most welcoming classroom spaces.

> In this classroom, we recognize that stories have power.
>
> We share the parts of our stories that we feel comfortable speaking and writing about.
>
> We are co-learners and can engage as speakers from our experiences when it feels right to do so.

# Visual Grammar

Bell presents the experience of learning how to navigate the world and how to explore language in visual/verbal ways (pp. 28–29), including instruction for how to lip-read and make use of visual clues. The book also normalizes the use of a hearing aid or assistive device, and I recognize that some members of the Deaf community do not depend on such devices. I further recognize that learning to read is often sound based but that literacy for individuals who are Deaf is a complex and beautiful process all its own, with the grammar of sign language and linking to pictures, gestures, and expressions. A visual grammar presented in this way is no less profound and amazing than a spoken or written one. I have worked with students who are Deaf at the university and middle school levels, and I learned much about how the reading process can work without sound systems when I was a doctoral student.

It can be helpful to recognize that American Sign Language (ASL) and other sign language dialects are, in fact, working languages, complete with a gestural grammar, and I appreciate ASL and other sign language systems as a linguistically powerful and meaningful way of communicating. In the times that I have been fortunate enough to work with students who are Deaf, I have gleaned much about the complexities of human experience and our use of language, and I have fond memories of negotiating what statements and expressions I could eliminate from class lectures in order to make the learning environment more welcoming for students and their interpreters.

## Classroom Application Ideas

One of the advantages of teaching English language arts is that educators can seize on existing narratives to prompt conversations that might otherwise seem tenuous, centering stories that are shared as spaces for learning more. With this approach, texts can serve as communal spaces for reflection and healing. Using specific texts has the power to open up opportunities to see into the lives of those who are both like readers and who challenge readers to think and see in new ways. Authors and artists can help educators broach topics in ways that feel more natural and convey positive messages in more inviting ways.

As I explore using *El Deafo* in instruction, I think about authors and readers creating a better and more inclusive world by pushing back on what conventions and expectations are in writing and composing and how these features are sometimes limiting. For each stage of this lesson sequence, I conclude with some lingering thoughts for teachers to explore with students. I also recommend the graphic novel *Mighty Jack* by Ben Hatke as a visual depiction of diverse abilities, as well as the Last Pick series by Jason Walz (interview featured at the end of this chapter). Both Last Pick and *Mighty Jack* portray characters on the autism spectrum in ways that encapsulate this experience as part of the narrative and emphasize the power of these characters. Moreover, characters in these books link with additional intersections of identity. *When Stars Are Scattered* features a character with diverse abilities, connecting to the books I have explored in this chapter and demonstrating yet another link that can be made through this graphic novel.

It is vital to find respectful representations of the experiences and abilities that are captured in books, and visual depictions can serve as rich sources for further discussion as students locate and create representations of themselves in visual and word-based forms. Characters with diverse abilities can, indeed, be the heroes of their own stories, showcasing the ways they experience the world as both a site of learning and agency. Though the character in *Stars* is not the central character/coauthor voice, there is a sense of love, care, and respect that comes through in the narrative.

## Step 1: Inviting Readers with the Graphic Novel

Before diving into the ideological and social work that a book like *El Deafo* or *When Stars Are Scattered* offers, I might begin a lesson sequence by previewing the text. As has been suggested, debates continue about the usefulness of graphic novels as "real" reading, with some authors and researchers suggesting that the books do indeed hold textual and invitational effect. It is my hope that this limiting narrative is changing more and more. Meanwhile, others express concern that teachers will rely more on the images offered in these books than the text they include. An effective instructional sequence featuring a graphic novel as a central text must make use of all aspects of the text, including the inferences that are made available in the visual work, and pay close attention to both text and word parts. When I teach Cece Bell's work, I offer this framework as a guiding essential question while also noting the power of representation in books like *El Deafo* to disrupt a deficiency model for reading instruction. Teachers can use the book and the author's experience as a foundation for talking about honoring the students in our classrooms who may learn in diverse ways or who may challenge our perspectives about what progress looks like.

From a multimodal perspective, teachers can work with students to consider both the images and text in graphic novels and picture books and can talk with students about the meanings that are conveyed by each one. Using language through assistive devices, for example, might be a one avenue of discussion as teachers unpack the use of symbols with students and the many ways communication can occur. Rather than viewing alternative systems of communication as lesser in any way, these discussions can be focused on rich opportunities for discovery, and teachers can center a range of types of response as "exemplary" when it comes to communicating in written and visual form.

As a reading teacher who also strives to be a good human, I know I have to pay attention to words and the ways they are used, including moments when labels create barriers rather than bridges between and among members within classroom communities. Moreover, as an educator who wishes to offer students experiences of success and engagement, I can also pause to discuss the other features offered in books like *El Deafo*. This text choice fits well at the upper elementary and middle grades level and offers opportunities for dialogue about how people are treated and represented.

### Lesson Prompt 1

How is *El Deafo* like books you have encountered before? What do you notice about how the author sets up the text? What words do you notice? What images stand out to you, and how do they add to your understanding? What effect do the words and pictures have on the story?

### Step 2: Closer Noticing

Once students have completed work with previewing this text, you might dig into this story. Without providing too much of the narrative content here, Bell has envisioned an animal-centered world in which she is a bunny-like character. Within this realm of fantasy, Bell uses the narrative to ask real-life questions and share about her experiences—even difficult ones. As with much of fantasy-oriented fiction, the story highlights aspects of our reality in ways that feel at once removed and relatable. What is a way that a student would wish to represent themselves in a story? Does a grounded visual of them feel appropriate, or do they wish to embody themselves in an alternative, fantastic way to (re)envision their areas of strength?

The reader is presented with this fantasy world and with Bell's experiences in school, but the links between fantasy and reality clearly hint at the memoir-driven nature of the book. This is where the social, emotional, and relational work of the book really begins and where themes of belonging and inclusion can be an area of particular focus. As we are told at the outset of the story, the main character is ready to move beyond labels, bringing to mind the way Stephanie Harvey and Annie Ward speak of tabling labels in their 2017 book *From Striving to Thriving: How to Grow Confident, Capable Readers*. While I am a proponent of using data to inform instruction, I am also careful to make sure my use of data is not limiting in any way and is thoughtful and asset- and strength-based. Harvey and Ward center this student-driven approach.

In further analysis, the graphic novel medium can allow readers to zoom in on certain features (for example, the book's gutters or spaces between panels) and highlight the meaning that is made on the page. By taking full advantage of a page's grammatical and semantic features, teachers create a model for what close, skilled reading looks like.

### Lesson Prompt 2

What do you think of this fantasy world? If you could imagine yourself as a superheroic/animal character, what would it be? In what ways is the setting in this graphic novel similar to and different from the world in which we live? How do you think the main character will change across the storyline?

## Step 3: Further Applications

As educators and humans, we know that readers have a variety of needs, and we also know that students have experienced and are experiencing many emotions and concerns. I acknowledge that the work of inclusivity is never done and that I am always improving. One concern teachers face is encouraging students to represent themselves in stories and to discover their sense of author identity in healthy, reflective, and affirming ways. Books like *El Deafo* show us the world around us in new ways and highlight a range of experiences so that we can collectively begin to see differences as superpowers. One way I like to think through this is to have students write three strengths about themselves. Neighboring students can help students to see themselves from an outside perspective as well. I also like to ask students to consider features they like about themselves.

When using *El Deafo* as a classroom text, engaging students in creating their own stories is a pedagogical and affirming possibility. Because the book uses words and pictures, students can be afforded more options in the ways they wish to share their experiences and more avenues to construct meaning. As is always the case, I suggest creating comfortable boundaries around this act of storytelling, and I would not require students to share any aspect of their lives with the class that they did not wish to publish. This is a clear link back to the classroom routines mentioned earlier in this chapter, a point of practical consistency.

There are also lesson possibilities with this book, as well as a wide variety of others, for locating the ways the ideas presented take shape in real life.

### Lesson Prompt 3

It's time to share about ourselves and explore more. Cece Bell shares a story of self and personal experience told in words and pictures. Please use words, pictures, or both to share your experiences. What does the book teach us about ourselves? How does this book reflect issues in the real world?

## Further Applications

As mentioned at the outset, *El Deafo* is a unique book in its design and also in that it is written by an author/artist with a first-person understanding of Deafness.

Beginning a unit focused on *El Deafo* or incorporating the book as a support text has continued possibilities as more parts of Bell's story unfold throughout the unit. It is perhaps the case that students may not immediately relate to the experiences of a person who is deaf, but teachers can point out additional aspects of experience and growth that all learners share.

## Next Steps in Instruction: *Mighty Jack* and More

As an additional text to examine, I suggest Ben Hatke's *Mighty Jack*. In classroom practice with a group of third graders in an online pandemic space, I found the need to draw particular attention to the ways that the brother/sister relationship is portrayed in this book as students were curious about these dynamics. Jack's sister, Maddy, is a character who is on the autism spectrum. Her role in the book, including her moments of silence, lead to possibilities for resonating with student experiences, as well as moments of inference in the text. As with wordless graphic novels and picture books, these moments of quiet with image-only panels create opportunities for examining character development as well as for making inferences and drawing attention to the ways that images work. Though Jack is the central character, Maddy's involvement in the story is arguably just as central. The reader is never informed about Maddy, specifically, but teachers and students can work together to draw these inferences and see the character not simply as a secondary foil but as a force who becomes active in the text.

Next, I recommend the graphic novel series Last Pick from author/artist Jason Walz. Walz is a special education teacher who imagines a world in which aliens have invaded and captured all of the people they believe pose a threat, leaving behind those who are very old, very young, or differently abled. The relationship between the two main characters, siblings Sam and Wyatt, is one of the elements of the book series, as is the presentation of autism. I admit a sense of bias when it comes to Walz's work—the way that he presents this fantasy/science-fiction world is open-ended, and only at the end of the book does the reader learn about the Walz's intentions and background with the work.

Both the Last Pick series and *Mighty Jack* contain a sense of adventure and would provide genre appeal for readers who enjoy science fiction and fantasy. Both Walz and Hatke include several notes to the world of sci-fi in their books, with both visual homages and in-text references noting other works. These aspects of genre can create a more instant engagement for young readers who enjoy stories like this, while a host of other graphic novels that speak to issues of inclusion, identity, and diversity can be implemented for readers who prefer other types of stories.

I also know that graphic novels and comics are media that are regarded as go-to resources for students who are receiving special-education services. This is noteworthy, and there are instances of students in special education who are able to demonstrate agency and expertise with comics (Reid & Moses, 2021). Comics are sometimes seen as an instructional scaffold for readers who are determined (Golding & Verrier, 2021). I love this narrative of comics as strengths-based texts of expertise; I also recognize that comics are complex in their compositional ontology (Cohn, 2018) and are also consumed by adult readers who point to them as endemic to their reading histories (Botzakis, 2009). This again reflects the flexible nature of comics as books that can offer support for readers as well as texts that can challenge and fascinate readers who are voracious consumers of a wide variety of texts.

As I work to improve my pedagogy and reflect on these questions, I offer a few questions for considering graphic novels that represent diverse abilities.

For readers who want to learn more about literacy in Deaf communities, I recommend the "15 Principles for Reading to Deaf Children" and other literacy resources from the Laurent Clerc National Deaf Education Center at Gallaudet University.

As promised, I conclude this chapter with an interview with Walz and recommend a teacher's guide for the books that are currently available on his website.

## Words from Jason Walz

*Please tell us about the inspiration for the Last Pick series (as seen in Figure 7.2).*
**Jason Walz**: So, I'm a special-education teacher, and most of my experience has been working with kids on the autism spectrum. I help older students in special education learn job skills, get jobs, and hopefully keep jobs. My job has been to hustle and talk to businesses in the community. My students are amazing— brilliant, interesting, creative, and clever. I've found that the United States does a really good job of creating laws that say everyone is equal, but not all businesses practice that. So, all these brilliant students I had kept getting told no constantly. I wanted to tell a story about people who are still pushed to the side, talking about people with disabilities in general. They are often treated as second-class citizens.

I wanted to tell a story that was super-fun, full of monsters, aliens, explosions, and adventure. I also don't want to be preachy, so I tried to sneak

**FIGURE 7.2.** Image Courtesy of Jason Walz

in what was important to me. It's about how we segregate people into groups of those deemed "worthy" and "unworthy." I wanted a story where those who are labeled unworthy find a place to stand up against oppressors. I worked with students in the writing of the characters to get the voice right, particularly people on the autism spectrum. Sometimes it's super-tricky. There are some tropes in storytelling that I wanted to avoid, and I wanted someone who has autism to be as authentic as possible, and I needed help with that. I'm a white, cis male, and I was lucky enough that there is a revolution in YA books and in comics. It was really important that I wasn't stealing someone else's voice. I had a great editor, and I had to do as much of my homework as I possibly could.

*How did you plan the series out?*
**Jason Walz**: I was initially thinking about it as a monthly comic. I was just writing it, and I did two issues on my own. Right around that time, I was in one of my school teacher meetings and got an email from an agent. At that point, the book series was called Uppercut. In that back and forth, the book shaped itself, and they gave ideas for how the series might look.

   As I was hearing all of that, the "what if" light comes on to shape the story. When it comes to popular culture, trilogies are ingrained in me. Thank you, *Star Wars*. So, I went with that right away. If you are interested in being a writer, there are a thousand ways to do it. Many people swear by independent publishing. The great thing is that the publisher can help to shape the work.

*How much of yourself and your story makes its way into your books?*

**Jason Walz**: I realize more and more that my personal life is in my writing, not even as a subtext. I can go back and see what I'm working through in plot and theme. I also have two boys. When I started *Last Pick*, I wanted a diverse cast of characters because I wanted my boys to grow up reading about different points of view and seeing different representations. I wanted them to see a brilliant, beautiful, powerful lead character who just happens to be female. I want to raise two boys who just do a good job in life. We really have to do good work. If we are going to put stuff out there as parents, I want to feel good about my kids reading it and that they will grow in some way. I think about them as readers.

# Black Joy, Black Lives Matter, and Antiracist Pedagogy in Graphic Novels

We have to work actively, and in public, every single day if we want to be culturally relevant, antiracist people and educators.

—KIMBERLY N. PARKER, *Literacy Is Liberation: Working Toward Justice Through Culturally Relevant Teaching,* p. 15

• *Learning for Justice—Identity Anchor Standard 5. Students will recognize traits of the dominant culture, their home culture, and other cultures and understand how they negotiate their own identity in multiple spaces.*

## Linking to and Listening to Experiences

As a white man, I recognize that my knowledge of authentic experiences with racism is limited; indeed, I have never experienced racism. At one time, I even thought that racism was a concept of the past, only relegated to particular social spaces and moments. I have since learned that our living reality is very different, and I began to reach this conclusion while teaching Harper Lee's *To Kill a Mockingbird* and noting the ways that my majority white students reacted to the text and talked about the conversations happening in their households.

While I may be able to speak to minoritization based on gender or class, there is a position of advocacy and allyship I take when it comes to talking about race that I attempt to work from, centering both the problematic history of the treatment of people of color in the United States as well as the notion of Black joy. Again, my conversation about this is very limited, but I position myself as a learner.

When I enter a classroom with a text by a Black author, I attempt to frame the reading experience as a consideration of the author/artist's story and not my own. It is their voice that I want to hear and share with students, and I am only a signpost and designer/acknowledger of open space for conversations to occur.

As Kimberly Parker (2022) noticed in her first year of teaching, there is no shortage of white-centered texts for students to read: "I knew I wanted my first group of freshmen to read, and I knew I needed lots of books. The ones I gathered were often from donation centers, featuring white characters doing white things" (p. 18). While Parker had collected some books focused on the experiences of people of color, there were "not nearly enough" (p. 18). This finding continues to be resonant when considering the number of texts that are available for a range of experiences, and yet classrooms are diverse places where many experiences and voices are present.

I hear this message from Parker loud and clear, and I strive to include books in my classes and courses that feature a range of cultural experiences from many authors and artists. Furthermore, I acknowledge the discomfort that talking about race and racism can create in the discussion that follows communal reading experiences while also acknowledging the need to include a wide range of stories in classroom libraries. What's more, these books are a central part of classroom reading practices, not simply appearing on our bookshelves but shared in the context of instruction for dialogue and learning. I also aim to be authentic in my conversations about these and other(ed) topics (and persons). As an educator, I know the language of equity and diversity, as well as inclusivity, very well; I want to do more than access a particular vocabulary. I want these practices to be evident down to the core of what I do as an educator.

The results are worth it, and the reality I embrace is worth it. After all, there are worse experiences than discomfort.

Building on this section's theme of graphic novels as sites for representation, I look at the work of Jerry Craft, particularly in his graphic novel *New Kid*.

## Brief Statement on the Relevance of *New Kid*

I would be remiss in writing a text about the flexibility of graphic novels without mentioning the 2019 Newbery-winning book *New Kid* (Craft, 2019). Craft makes beautiful and stunning use of the comics medium, illustrating how the main character, Jordan, experiences navigating the presentation of self to the world around him. Jordan is a new kid, as advertised in the title, who goes to a private school and encounters friendships, microaggressions, and all the challenges of middle school life. This centering of race and ethnicity as an interwoven aspect of the main character's being, alongside a beautiful narrative, dovetails with Jamieson and Mohamed's work in *When Stars Are Scattered*. It is neither an add-on to the book, didactically appearing as an end itself, nor is race and ethnicity presented as the sole focus on the book. Rather, the character is presented as a Black youth in the same way that a teacher might encounter a child in the classroom. Jordan just is who he is, and the book is both fun at many turns and thought-provoking.

As I explore the graphic novel with students, I point to many components; namely, *New Kid* carries with it the Newbery distinction, which is worth mentioning to students (and families) who have questions about the "real book" nature of the comics medium. To reiterate, comics and graphic novels are, indeed, real books. This alone can and should act as a step for buy-in with critics of comics.

Additionally, there are unique opportunities for teaching and engaging contained in the graphic novel. Craft includes nods to experiences of being Black in ways that are authentic and humanly shared. His stories focus on the lives of children who are experiencing the world around them, and readers are taken along on this journey. This author/artist includes cultural references that readers can appreciate both in the text of his books as well as in the chapter dividers. In *New Kid*, these dividers are references to film and popular culture; in the second book, *Class Act*, they are references to popular graphic novels. I confess that my first reading of *New Kid* took place in one sitting. I stayed up late to finish the book and adored the ways that it drew upon superhero stories and real life, and how it wove in elements of popular culture with insightful commentary. I knew the first time I read this book that I wanted to use it in instruction, and I have since incorporated it in five courses.

## Close Looks

Simple activities like catching the bus are presented in layered and considerate experiences of enacting dress and manner for a Black youth. Across six panels and two pages (Craft, 2019, pp. 56–57), Jordan demonstrates a verbal and visual explanation of his need to be chameleonic in daily travels, from a hoodie-up and sunglasses-wearing approach (p. 56, panel A) to dropping his hoodie (p. 56, panel B) to removing his sunglasses (p. 56, panel C). From there, Jordan makes further augmentations in his conversation and manner, with the effect being a sense of exhaustion.

For Jordan, negotiating daily life carries many of the questions and concerns that all kids consider, alongside the added burden of attempting to fit in and make others around him feel safe and, consequently, contribute to his own feeling of belonging and safety.

Jordan is not presented as a one-dimensional character. He has relatable likes and interests, as well as social experiences that upper elementary, middle grades, and high school students will find links with. The fact that Jordan is a Black youth is essential yet crafted as an aspect of his social being and person that does not feel emblematic or shallow. The graphic novel offers a first-person subjective narration in visual form that is so often only found in film in this regard. We, the reader, have the opportunity to peek inside Jordan's notebook, seeing the sketches he creates as the world unfolds around him with all of its limitations and troublesome treatment of Black youth in a mostly white school.

Comics scholars have already begun to unpack *New Kid* in terms of its semiotics and its classroom and textual implications (Boerman-Cornell & Kim, 2020). There is still much to explore in the book as well as in its sequel. Teachers can ask a range of questions with the text, from the surface-level inquiries about characters and settings to questions of how the text connects with other readings and real-life experiences. Craft has a way of establishing settings and characters through panels that is a ready-made step to link to standards focused on plots and narratives.

## Texts That Miss the Mark

When it comes to issues of race and racism, we can think about both the use of language and the ways that experience is portrayed. Speaking as an observer/outsider when it comes to this topic, I note that discussion of ethnic, racial, and cultural identity should include both a realistic and full depiction of the history of Black communities, including but certainly not limited to narratives of persons who have been enslaved; what's more, I suggest moving discussion to areas of Black joy. As Craft's novel relates, stories of Black experiences are not always urban tales of grittiness, and focusing on stories of woe from a historical and literary perspective is only one dimension of what teachers can share. For more on the concept of Black joy, see the work of Bettina Love. I also especially recommend Dunn and Love's 2020 research—these authors point to the incomplete nature of pedagogy without a focus on Black joy.

In contrast to the rounded depiction of Jordan, presentations of Black comics characters, particularly in the superhero comics of the 1960s and on, are often one-dimensional, and Black heroes are often relegated to a secondary focus as sidekicks. Black heroes are also sometimes presented as former criminals (see, the *Black Lightning* origin story in DC Comics, as well as Marvel's *Luke Cage: Hero for Hire*).

A singular view of identity can be severely limiting, as can an avoidance of authors and stories of color by teachers and readers in general. The notion of not seeing color fails to help us engage in the critical work of looking at who and what we celebrate and share about both through classroom curriculum and the books that educators choose to include as part of instruction beyond curriculum.

## Classroom Application Ideas

In exploring stories that highlight characters of a range of experiences and ethnicities, I suggest a cultural panoply or multimodal approach that includes real objects (realia) and artistic reaction so that students can physically put into place the ideas they explore. In Figure 8.1, a student explores dimensions of experience through a three-dimensional painted cube; in Figure 8.2, a student explores intersections of identity in reflective reading through a crocheted piece.

In this assignment, students chose a reading from a list of curated texts and also had the opportunity to propose a text that was not on the list. As the teacher, I attempted to choose a number of books on the recommendation list that stemmed from authentic experiences. Students then read the book they chose over the course of about one month with reflections and questions along the way. One week's goal was to create a response to their reading up to that point and, in addition to the traditional written response, I made space for a range of multimodal creations.

When granted freedom to explore avenues of creation, students can explore aspects of their identities, including ethnicity, language, and culture, through sharing about parts of their lived experiences in project-based options. The multimodal mosaic approach can be implemented as a next step beyond an identity web, in which students would write a list about parts of their lives and favorite activities, using words and pictures. In all truth, allowing for this kind of choice-based response is a joy to explore in terms of grading and responding as the teacher as well, and it allows such a varied set of student-created products.

**FIGURE 8.1.** Student-Created Multimodal Product (Cube)

A multimodal approach can invite creation across images, words, and digital texts. These can include audio clips, music, and video clips, and can feature a presentation of what parts of life students consider most salient in their intersections of identity. This work can begin with young children and need not be held off for upper elementary or secondary instruction, where it might be more commonly found. I cannot assume that I know the experiences of everyone in any given classroom; in fact, I recognize that students of color have likely faced or are facing racism, and there are nuances of experience to consider. I also recognize that this conversation is about more than choosing particular texts; it reaches into the kinds of environments I create and sustain as a teacher.

**FIGURE 8.2.** Student-Created Multimodal Response (Crochet)

The caveat that comes with this kind of approach is that I would not encourage students to act as speakers for a particular lived experience—a practice that is problematic and places on students a burden that might be confusing and stressful. Rather, I suggest that visual and verbal stories about experiences should inspire us to share our own stories and experiences. This, once more, is optional, and I do not ask students to speak as members representing entire groups.

I seek to create classroom environments with students as well as places where students can freely explore the intersections of their identities and real-life questions and issues. As students explore, I emphasize that they should only disclose what they want, when they want, and in the way that is most comfortable for them. Comics are ideal mentor texts for multimodal products that allow for exploring multilingual and multicultural experiences across many modes. While comics are themselves used as central texts in my classes, the examples above illustrate the ways that I try to invite creation beyond the printed or digital page.

When it comes to student journaling, I do not assume that I am the sole audience. Rather, I want to encourage students to engage in the practice of writing openly. Their choice to share writing with me is part of their autonomy in the process. When they do share, it is an honor to be part of that process and to be an audience to their story, and my feedback first focuses on their voice and the power of their story before I ever begin to think about linking writing to lessons about grammar and conventions.

## Steps for Further Work (Including Additional Resources/Book Titles)

Beyond creation, teachers can always point to critical reading to consider the voices that are centered in narratives, as well as those that have been removed. I am keen to note texts that might be triggering because of racialized/demeaning language, and I seek texts that offer more than tragedy and stories that portray people of color in one dimension or as lacking agency in any way. I am particularly drawn to stories in which the main characters, regardless of their racial identities, are active forces for change.

*Nubia: Real One* is another such graphic novel text. Published by DC Comics in 2021, the book is written by L. L. McKinney and drawn by Robyn Smith. Nubia is a Black Amazon, from the same community as Wonder Woman. Acting as a stand-alone entry in a DC young-adult graphic-novel series, the character is presented in a contemporary environment as a teenager grappling with the desire to protest and make change in her world as well as critically reflecting on the way that the world reacts to her based on the color of her skin. I also recommend *Mister Miracle: The Great Escape* by Varian Johnson (2022), as well as his graphic novel *Twins* (2020). Additionally, a number of popular culture stories, from Spider-Man to the Tolkien universe, have begun to more thoughtfully include characters from diverse ethnic and racial backgrounds. Discussing these media-oriented texts with students can be either a foundation or a continuing thread in thinking about how representation occurs in stories, and this can lead to work on both critical reading and viewing.

As further resources on antiracist pedagogy, I recommend a variety of texts, both for student reading and for building teacher awareness, and I should note that I am still reading and learning as well. Though not technically a graphic novel, I recommend exploring *This Book Is Antiracist* by Tiffany Jewell and Aurelia Durand (2020) as a layered and visually stunning exploration of race, ethnicity, and intersections of identity. Many of my students have commented on the graphic novel-like quality of the book and have posed critical questions of systems of power based on our classroom discussions that stem from the book.

This informational text includes writing activities as well as a glossary of helpful terms for readers who are new to exploring antiracism. I also suggest the picture books *Antiracist Baby* by Ibram X. Kendi and Ashley Lukashevsky (2020) and *Black Is a Rainbow Color* by Angela Joy and Akua Holmes (2020) as powerful visual avenues for exploring antiracist education and Black joy. Holmes's work, in particular, is an invitation to further considerations for making, including the possibilities of creating comics from collage-like work, rather than relying on illustrations for each panel.

*Swim Team* by Johnnie Christmas (2022) is another wonderful graphic novel that explores Black history and identity seen in the life of a young Black girl who wants to be part of the swim team. Part of this graphic novel explores the history of segregation in public pools.

The artistic work that is featured in *New Kid,* namely Jordan's notebook, can act as a mentor text within the larger network of text in the graphic novel, inspiring young readers to engage in writing and drawing—and perhaps inspiring teachers to develop invitations to writing centered around the topics that are important to Jordan. Additionally, I recommend Craft's 2020 *Comic Relief* contribution to *The New York Times,* "A Marvel-ous Reader," in which he briefly shares some of his literacy history as someone who engaged with the comics medium and found much to enjoy and learn from it, including the wide range of science words employed in Marvel Comics.

Here are some other works by scholars of color who can point to experiences of Black joy and ideas about critical pedagogy in impactful and authentic ways:

*We Want to Do More Than Survive: Abolitionist Teaching and the Pursuit of Educational Freedom* by Bettina Love (2020). Love points to experience in teaching, as well as scholarship, to contend for social change while taking a close look at the brokenness of systems of power.

*Cultivating Genius: An Equity Framework for Culturally and Historically Responsive Literacy* by Gholdy Muhammad (2020). Muhammad offers a pedagogical framework that includes criticality as well as development of identity, proficiencies, and knowledge.

*Reading, Writing, and Racism: Disrupting Whiteness in Teacher Education and in the Classroom* by Bree Picower (2021). Picower examines curricular approaches and examples of inequity reproduced in instructional and assessment practices. Of particular note within the scope of this book, the author presents a critique of the presentation of characters in comics and calls for more diversity in the medium.

*The Dark Fantastic: Race and the Imagination from* Harry Potter *to the*

Hunger Games by Ebony Elizabeth Thomas (2020). This text explores the presentation of Black character in popular stories, particularly in fantasy and science fiction. The stories are considered across media.

For older readers, I suggest the book *Artie and the Wolf Moon* by Olivia Stephens (2021) as a story that is fantasy-/horror-driven, and as another example of a graphic novel that centers Black characters. Stephens is the artist on the graphic novel adaptation of *Tristan Strong Punches a Hole in the Sky* (Mbalia, 2020), and an interview with this author and artist serves as a final section for this chapter.

## Words from Olivia Stephens

*Please tell us about the inspiration behind your creative work.*
**Olivia Stephens:** I get inspired by a lot of things: nature, history, my personal observations, music. Everything that I absorb or encounter in my life feeds into how I might tell a story. And that's true for everyone. No ideas are "original" these days, but the way someone tells a story and what they choose to focus on in their telling can make their perspective unique from others.

*What would you like to tell us about your creative process?*
**Olivia Stephens**: My stories often start with a premise or a "what if?" question. And because I often write supernatural stories, the "what if" tends to be an otherworldly element dropped into an otherwise normal world. Those scenarios excite me, and I like to ponder on how I (or a character I made up) might react to a supernatural situation. From there, I tend to make a playlist of music to listen to while I work out the rest of the story in my head. A lot of the time, the playlist is a way for me to figure out what the tone of a story is and where I'm trying to take things emotionally. I don't feel comfortable moving forward until the emotional heart of a premise rings true. I can't really explain it more than that. It's a very organic and intuitive process for me.

*What draws you to the graphic novel/comics medium?*
**Olivia Stephens:** I feel like I'm able to say everything I need to say with comics. I've tried to write strict prose in the past but always felt constrained because there were parts of a story I could only communicate with images. Once I came around to making my own comics, everything clicked into place. For me, it feels like a complete language that is primed for experimentation between word and image.

*I love the way you include supernatural elements and realistic characters—how do you decide what goes into the work you do?*

**Olivia Stephens:** I enjoy working with supernatural elements in realistic settings because, as I said earlier, I love to speculate about how one might realistically navigate unbelievable situations. It also feels more comfortable to tackle subjects that are close to my heart when I'm able to obfuscate them via the fantastical. It grants me some emotional distance to work out feelings that are otherwise too raw for me to approach. I don't really want to make work about myself (because my life is fairly boring); I'd rather write about the adventures of strangers and add in some personal touches so that they feel a little more familiar to me.

*What is the message you'd like to send through Artie and the Wolf Moon?* (See Figure 8.3)

**Olivia Stephens:** Besides just trying to tell an interesting story, I hope that readers find *Artie and the Wolf Moon* an empowering story. There is a lot of darkness in the world. But when you

**FIGURE 8.3.** Image Courtesy of Olivia Stephens

find the people in your life who love you and only want to help you become the best possible version of yourself that you can be, anything is possible.

# Adding Words, Exploring Language: Stories of (Im)migration and Removal in Graphic Novels

- *Learning for Justice—Diversity Anchor Standard 10. Students will examine diversity in social, cultural, political, and historical contexts rather than in ways that are superficial or oversimplified.*

In this chapter, I offer a lesson idea that focuses on wordless books as well as the range of stories of immigration, migration, and removal. I have sometimes assumed this set of experiences to be one-dimensional, yet I have learned about stories of removal that have occurred and continue to occur in the real world that are anything but.

When it comes to graphic novels of (im)migration experiences, I can think of no greater example than *When Stars Are Scattered* for exploring this range of experiences in the comics format from an authentic voice. This is perhaps the strongest link with the text, and I would be remiss not to note this aspect of the book. In a recent middle grades methods course, students had the chance to choose a graphic novel to read, and I was pleased to see that *Stars* was a top choice.

Though *When Stars Are Scattered* is a signpost throughout this book, I centralize this text in this chapter and discuss it as a culturally and experientially original and authentic text that can lead to critical conversations. I am also thinking about the links between this text and Shaun Tan's *The Arrival*, another book that fascinates my students.

*The Arrival* (2007) has been the subject of previous research (Bjartveit & Panayotidis, 2014; Dallaqua et al., 2014; Farrell et al., 2010). The book is a linking of real-life images and fantasy depiction, as evidenced on the cover: a traveler encountering a mythical creature. The traveler is the central character, and the experience of removal is illustrated through the book's wordless pages.

Tan presents a juxtaposition of comfort and mysticism, the fantasy creatures embodying dangers and wonders unknown. This is a discussion-worthy visual representation of the uncertainty of being removed and the fears that come alongside such an experience. Even the language features of the book, from the very beginning, present the title and author name in an unfamiliar typography; we, the reader, encounter these features transliterated back to English on the following title page. The reader is then presented with a nine-panel arrangement of familiar objects with the central image being a child's drawing of a family with joyful expressions. Tan's rendering of the family is then seen again in the lower-right corner of the page.

A teapot, cup and saucer, clothing, clock, and other objects create a sense of home. Linking directly to the notion of travel right away, Tan depicts a family photograph being wrapped and packed on the next page in a similar layout. While the first page is a nine-panel presentation of different artifacts and objects, the following layout is a nine-panel presentation of the process of preparing to leave. Arguably, the central emotional dichotomy of the book is presented in these two pages and then expanded on over the course of the visual narrative.

I have included a set of lesson steps that I recommend for *The Arrival* through guiding questions in Figure 9.1. Linking back to the notion of the mythical/feature creature, the shadow of a dragon tail is seen on the wall behind the family as they leave, in full-page (splash page) format (Tan, 2006, p. 5). In the following spread, the image is expanded on in a cityscape view. Were this a film, this would be an establishing location shot with the dragon tail entwining among the structures.

## Lesson Protocol/ Questions for *The Arrival*

1. Cover and title page: What elements of language and travel do you see? Why do you think Shaun Tan begins the story with these designs?

2. Opening pages: What is the significance of the nine-frame arrangement of objects on the first page?

3. Inference points: Why are we encountering these images? How do they relate to the images of packing that we see next?

4. Close focus: What does each family member/character feel? What clues can we see in their expressions?

5. Inference point: Why is the family leaving?

**FIGURE 9.1.** Lesson Questions for Tan's Work

I have shared this book with several groups of students, and there has been a consistent response to the text. Sometimes students comment that they find the images haunting and engaging but sometimes confusing. In a first-year composition class in 2018, a student who had emigrated from Russia as a young person vividly engaged with the book by recounting memories of visiting Chernobyl as a child, describing the metallic taste of strawberries, while a student recently commented on the shadow characters and visions that are part of the story.

## Expanding on Possibilities with Wordless Books

While scholars like Barbara Postema and Frank Serafini have written about the potential for using wordless books with young readers, what I offer in this chapter is a step-by-step reflection on work with these books with readers in face-to-face and virtual teaching. Postema rightly points to the differences between traditional children's books and this form as well as the cognitive demand that is created by using these books.

I advocate for a close reading of the books guided by teacher inquiry and discussion. Discussion can include stopping and writing as well. While reading a graphic novel may seem like simple work, there are actually many steps in thinking about the role of words and text, and it has been suggested that teachers think carefully about instructional steps with graphic novels (Chase et al., 2014; Golding & Verrier, 2021).

When it comes to introducing the world of comics and graphic novels, wordless books may prove to be an interesting source for readers and can certainly draw attention to the visuals. In a recent interview with comics scholar Nick Sousanis, the use of Sara Varon's *Robot Dreams* formed a common thread in pedagogical practice as an example of a text to draw readers into the form. The initial attention only to words can be mitigated by providing students with a page that includes only images. As noted, while scholars have written about wordless picture books, wordless graphic novels have not been written about extensively outside of book reviews.

In a course focused on literacy assessment, this type of book is often where this work begins when showcasing visual texts. In classroom collaboration, using wordless graphic novels provides an opportunity to take reading into unexpected territory. What I have discovered in this assessment course, and what I continue to reflect on, is the power of a misunderstood and often-diminished medium to engage readers and writers of all ages—not because they *can't* read and write, but because they might be interested in other kinds of books and ways of communicating. You can see a student-created example in Figure 9.2.

# Adding Words
# to the Wordless Comic

Wordless books, whether they are classified as picture books, comics, or graphic novels, can be intriguing reading experiences (particularly for close reading of images) while also presenting challenges for a teacher who is not familiar with how to build instruction from them. I suggest using sticky notes or index cards to create words to add to the page. I am an avid annotator when it comes to most texts, but the comics page simply does not seem like the page for additional scribbling. Notably, when working with students who have experienced (im) migration, the use of a particular language is not as important as the experience of engaging with the texts. I see this as an opportunity to invite young readers and writers to generate texts in a way that is most comfortable for them—a potentially ripe learning experience for the educator as well.

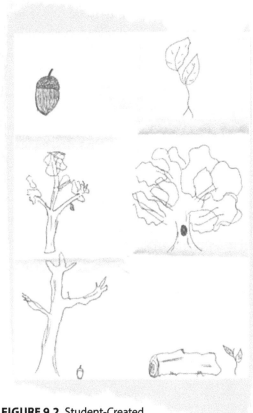

**FIGURE 9.2.** Student-Created Wordless Example

## Day One: Noticing

When we begin reading *The Arrival*, I note that a wordless graphic novel creates challenges and yet affords much for a young reader. First, there may be the need to attend to some of the words that occur naturally in context in the book.

In some ways, these words found in Tan's fictional environment mimic real life, as a reader might encounter terms without really needing to attend to them. What is of interest in *The Arrival* is the complexity and beauty of the images that Shaun Tan uses. As teachers introduce this book, a guiding question for students might be, "What do you notice?" I use this question often when I teach visual literature (as well as any kind of text). A "noticing" question is low-stakes and invites dialogue even from the corners of the room that are often quiet, as students have experienced less than positive moments of success with question-answer-response types of discussion centered on details or surface elements of particular texts.

As follow-up questions in a small group or even in whole-class instruction, teachers might ask what students notice on particular pages, and why they think the author made some of the choices that they did. In this way, educators are opening up experiences with the book. For readers who are still making progress, my hunch is that many of their experiences with text so far have been stressful. Linking points in the book are particularly salient for this work, as when the reader is first introduced to the shadow creature in *The Arrival* or when Sara Varon first makes a transition between reality and dreaming in *Robot Dreams* (accomplished through the use of a wavy panel line rather than a straight one—a graphic novel feature that, admittedly, I had to reread in order to notice).

My desire as I craft a lesson is always to be inviting and to disrupt student expectations of struggle, and my desire is also that students can come to view storytelling and their personal stories in different ways. For some readers, an experience with a graphic novel might be the first positive experience they have had with a book in quite some time—or at all.

As seen in Figure 9.3, questioning and breaking apart a text is critical and thoughtful work. In this example, I first began noting questions on sticky notes as I read the text. I then crafted questions in more detailed form as models for the preservice teachers I was working with as they thought about using the text to engage with children in their classrooms. Questions appear on the left while additional notes about particular moments in the text and links to crafting questions for providing metacognitive moments appear on the right-hand side. Additionally, I include annotations as I think and rethink the presentation of the material. These layers of examination and practice are a ready-made example for pre-service teachers to see that instruction is a multiple-step process and one that involves close attention to text, thinking through questions and lesson ideas, and changing instructional techniques when needed.

## Day Two: Facilitating the Discussion

Once students have encountered the text through a series of questions and conversation points to draw their attention to parts of the page, the next instructional move is to ask them further questions about the design features of the book. Often, graphic novels open with a splash page, which is a full-page picture. After that, graphic novels and comic books typically offer a story that is broken into panels. I might consider showing traditional examples of comics, often found in work published by Dark Horse Comics, DC Comics, and Marvel Comics, before guiding students through a text that works differently.

Gosh, I'm starting to think there are no words at all in this book, or at least very few. What do you think is happening on page 10? Does this remind you of anything you've done before?

*[handwritten: what do you like about that part?]*

What words do you think would go on this page? What would the characters say? Do you think they get along?

By page 10, I am recognizing that Sara has set up a two-character structure for this story. She is doing visual characterization, mostly through showing what the robot and dog are doing. So, she's building a foundation for the start of this friendship. If you want to connect to standards, you can start to ask about themes, but I would actually wait until a little further into the book, or maybe even save that for the end. You start asking about themes and too many literary devices, and we've stopped enjoying the book and we're just doing test prep.

*We can skip ahead a bit here for the sake of time and clarity.*

At this point, I can do some writing and modeling with the student, or I can continue letting them do the scripting. I think it's great, if they're willing, to let them have the pen. Otherwise, I can take up the charge and do some writing, or I can just keep it all dialogic.

What do you think has happened on page 19? Sara is taking us back to the single image on the page again. Why do think she's doing that? *[handwritten: → pg. 20]*

I would continue this way for some time until…page 19. The narrative largely works with this kind of exposition-building about the characters. It's like two best friends until we get to this page.

Hmmm. What do you think the robot is doing on page 23? How do you know/how did you figure that out?

Here, dog encounters a problem. Robot has leapt into the sea and (science lesson) metal and water don't mix. Robot is frozen and dog has a choice. *[handwritten: Moral dilemma?]*

**FIGURE 9.3.** Sample Teacher Thinking and Questioning for *Robot Dreams*

In *The Arrival*, Tan follows this design convention, depending on the demands of the story, with full-page spreads and paneled presentations alternating throughout the book. These authorial/artistic choices are places where teachers might ask students a range of questions, as recommended in the box below.

1. Why is this page design different from the ones before it?

2. Why do you think the author/artist created the page this way?

3. What do you think the author/artist wants us to notice?

4. In what ways does the choice of the author/artist convey particular meanings?

5. What do you think the author/artist wants us to feel or learn from this page?

6. How can I use some of these techniques in my writing and composing?

**FIGURE 9.4.** Questions of Authorial/Artistic Choices.

As a class digs further into the narrative, there are times when the story takes different turns as the characters embark on travels and navigate challenges (see also the moments when the reader is taken into dreams and memories in Sara Varon's *Robot Dreams*). Such transitional sequences call for close attention and close reading, even in the absence of words. Arguably, it is this wordlessness that makes the book so powerful for close noticing, and the authorship of students can be centered; their individual experiences and interpretations of what is happening in the text can be drawn upon to create responses that draw on and extend what is on the page. In other words, if a comic (or any book) lacks words or has an aspect that appears to be dangling, as with an ending that is not quite neat and tidy, these are ready-made opportunities for students to engage in responding. I recommend, when possible, sharing these responses with the authors of the book themselves.

If teachers do not attend to these features, students could be lost in a narrative that might be nonlinear or difficult to follow. So, the work done in facilitating discussion is pointing out the way the author uses narrative boxes, called panels, and how these are designed to indicate moments when the story is told in a dream pattern. Though it might seem like inching along through the text, zooming in on each panel and taking note of what each section of the page offers is important work to do. I know as a new teacher, I was often guilty of moving way too quickly through a text. Even in a book that is assumed to be intuitive, our guiding steps can be helpful.

Even though readers will not be encountering technical terms and extensive vocabulary in a wordless graphic novel, books like *The Arrival* still offer much to grapple with for comprehension, not to mention further links to conversation. An older reader who has textual experience but who lacks confidence and perhaps some foundational reading skills may be more inclined to engage with a conversation about a book like this, leading to more and more experiences with literacy from a positive framing and a budding relationship with text.

Readers need to see themselves represented in books; readers also need to see themselves as readers.

## Day Three: Writing Our Visual Stories

Because I firmly believe that reading leads to writing and vice versa, the final day or phase of working with students would be to add words to the text. I like to use sticky notes to do this work in graphic novels so that annotations can be moved around and don't take away from the images and text the author has created.

This work follows from previous research with the book as well as with other wordless graphic novels. Teachers can begin by asking students what words they would like to add to the page and might model this at first by adding their own words and soliciting student feedback. Notably, the words added on the page can be dialogic, or they can exist in other ways in relationship to the text, including descriptions and narrative voice. A range of responses is possible.

In this way, the teacher has moved from a comprehension-rich discussion to giving students authorship and ownership over the reading event. From here, teachers might spend time, including an additional day if needed, inviting students to create their own stories using animals, creative settings, and fantasy characters. The challenge would be for students to begin with the images they want to create (or even locate in other texts) to cut out and paste in and then to add words when needed to help their audience build understanding of the story. Figure 9.5 illustrates one step-by-step approach to using wordless comics with intention.

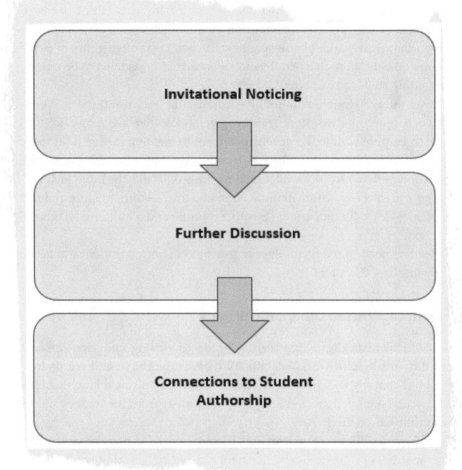

**FIGURE 9.5.** Steps in the Plan, Wordless or Otherwise

## Accommodations for the Plan

What takes three days may also be truncated to work over the course of three phases, depending on the time that can be dedicated to the lesson, or it can be extended to take up additional writing features and compositional steps. Teachers may also find that they need to offer more support at key moments in the narrative, as the story is nonlinear and involves a great deal of emotion and empathy. Some educators I have met collectively build graphic novel products over the course of an entire semester with work presented at the end that draws upon all of the material in a summative approach. Other educators take steps that are more like my own: with frequent writings that allow for responses to particular texts in particular moments. In other words, this plan can be shortened or extended as needed and based on the interests and needs of students. What I advocate for is engagement and conversation with students rather than a particular time frame. The timing of the lesson and activities can always be adjusted, and this largely depends on the group the teacher is working with as well as other external demands and features. If the process of reading a wordless graphic novel takes more time, is broken up over weeks, or is even more independent for students, all of this is acceptable and should meet the needs of teachers and students.

In the case of independent reading, I further advocate for checking in with students and inquiring about the text and what the reading was like. Part

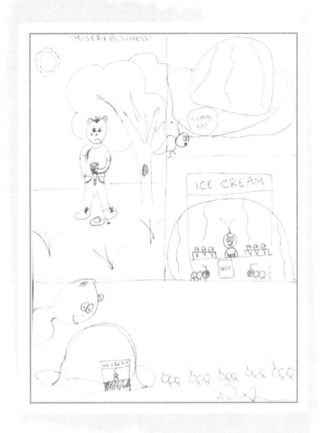

**FIGURE 9.6.** Student-Created Example with Limited Words

of the work that a wordless graphic novel affords is the deep conversation to fill the picture-oriented panels. For advanced learners, further analysis can be done with the images, and this may lead to creating a comic book/ graphic novel product as a class project. When possible, leading to steps of creation is a hallmark of strong pedagogy. Figure 9.6 shows an example of a mostly wordless comics page.

In some of the courses I have taught, the wordless graphic novel serves as an initial reading encounter or as the first in a series of lesson plans based on graphic novels that work in a ladder fashion to expose students to more complex reading. I also note the need at times to change lesson plans and approaches once they are started in response to evolving student needs. The work of education is artistic in nature and constantly reflective and reflexive as teachers make adjustments both in the moment and as a result of later thinking.

As a closing example, I recently shared pages from a similar wordless activity in an online virtual class with about 70 students. While I anticipated responses as I worked with preservice teachers, when I presented these pages, I found new opportunities for clarification that I had not anticipated. Some of this came from cultural background work as readers encounter images in different ways. Rather than see this as a problem in the lesson, I worked with a co-teacher to invest in these moments as fascinating opportunities to learn more about the perceptions of students. Other examples of potential barriers in instruction might include a perceived overreliance on picture cues with additional attention drawn to some of the incidental print that occurs in the book. Because of both the picture-story and the word-story elements of the book, teachers can draw fully on both systems of narrative to help students make connections.

Such is the ongoing work of shaping classroom practice and the need for flexibility and adjustment within practice when responses go "off-script." This is why reflection and continued practice and learning is so important in our work as educators.

## Questions for Reflection and Application

1. What are my assumptions about the comics medium?
2. Where might I begin instruction using visual texts?
3. What kinds of questions can I brainstorm to include in lessons focused on wordless graphic novels?
4. How can I build my stamina for closely reading a wordless graphic novel page with students?

### Additional Steps to Flex Your Graphic Novel Reading "Muscles"

1. Take note of your reading across pages. Are you focusing on the words or the pictures?
2. Reflect on your experience reading a book like *The Arrival*. How is this process different from other reading experiences? How might students find invitation or difficulty in a wordless page?
3. Think through and consider script moments where you might pause, notice, and ask questions with your students.

# Additional Texts Exploring (Im)migration Experiences

**TABLE 9.1.** Table of Additional Texts

| Title/Author | Brief Synopsis | Features |
|---|---|---|
| *Illegal* by Eoin Colfer and Andrew Donkin | The story of a young boy who sets out from Ghana on a journey to find his brother and sister and to make his way to Europe. | The book is powerfully and emotionally illustrated. Though it is fiction based on fact, the narrative is impactful. Along with *The Unwanted*, the book offers realistic and visual depictions of hard-hitting events. |
| *The Unwanted: Stories of the Syrian Refugees* by Don Brown | In an episodic and journalistic format, Don Brown depicts the plight of refugees attempting to flee Syria. | The YALSA Excellence in Nonfiction Winner, this book is jarring in its content (as is *Illegal*). Both of these books contain a degree of realism and loss as well as violence. |
| *Sea Prayer* by Khaled Hosseini (picture book) | Told through striking images and the poetic text that is so often found in a picture book, *Sea Prayer* is a message from a father to a son. | I recommend this as a picture book-adjacent text for a unit of stories of (im)migration. Characters face the challenges of memory and loss. |
| *Other Words for Home* by Jasmine Warga (verse novel) | Jude is a young girl whose experience of traveling from Syria to the United States is presented in verse, including the ways she navigates youth culture and questions of belonging. | I recommend this as a verse novel-adjacent text for a unit of stories of (im)migration. The main character, Jude, is both coming of age and coming to terms with Islamophobia and loss. |

## Additional Wordless Recommendations

As suggested in this chapter, I recommend building classroom conversations around wordless texts—this is where much of their linguistic power can be found. The sheer number of words that children can generate through insights about these books positions them as a deceptively "wordy" kind of reading. What's more, the lack of words in the texts can be more inviting for students who are moving toward English-language proficiency through another language.

Words are largely incidental in wordless graphic novels. Some terms appear in margins and backgrounds in Sara Varon's *Robot Dreams*, for example, but are not moved to the forefront of the reading experience. This presentation allows for a heightened awareness of what Varon is doing with the images themselves and also affords for dialogue with students about the meaning they are making on the page. Varon even includes images of texts that have inspired her work, which can be developing directions in further reading.

In Ben Hatke's *Little Robot*, many of the letters that appear on the page form guttural sounds and expressions from characters, sounds that are more emotional or visceral, rather than conveying strings of meaning in traditional sentences. Again, the effect is increasing awareness of what the artist/author is doing through the work of the image.

These pages can be excellent primers for helping our undergraduate and graduate preservice and inservice teachers to think about how reading visual text may be different and how they even call for a different level of attention than the meaning-making that takes place on a traditional book page.

The result that I have arrived at in the context of an assessment course is a sequence of graphic literature that could be used to support readers at a variety of levels and interests. In this chapter, the focus has been on a set of lesson steps that can be implemented with *The Arrival*. The agelessness of this sequence is

Words, Images, & Worlds with Andy Runton

**FIGURE 9.7.** An Image from a Full Audio/Video Interview with Andy Runton, Available at https://www.youtube.com/watch?v=W9E4DVZiuLg

part of its attractiveness for teachers, and it can be applied to wordless graphic novels that are aimed at younger audiences, including Andy Runton's Owly series. To conclude this chapter, Andy Runton was kind enough to share words for an interview about his authorship, as seen in Figure 9.7.

## An Interview with Andy Runton

*Owly is such an inviting series for young readers. How did the series come to be?*

**Andy Runton:** I grew up loving comics. I've always loved owls and drawing, but Owly started out as a simple little doodle on a Post-it note. When I was in college, I lived at home, and I would stay up really late working on design projects. I would leave little notes for my mom and let her know what time I went to bed, and it was always late, so she called me her little owl. She's always loved my cute little drawings—the cuter, the better. So, I drew this little owl on the notes to make her smile. But I drew him for years, and after a while he sort of became my mascot. Years later when I was trying to come up with a comic book idea, I tried everything, dragons, aliens, ninjas... nothing worked. Then one day I just looked at Owly and saw what I had. He had his own group of friends, and I loved drawing him. It all just unfolded. He had been there all the time, and I had missed him. After that, I started writing Owly stories and everything just clicked.

*What is your creative process like?*

**Andy Runton:** It takes me quite a while to create a book from start to finish. The hardest part is coming up with a story and then developing all of the elements and events that have to work together. The story is the most important part. Without it, everything crumbles. I discuss the story with my closest friends and editors. Once I have the basics down, I jot out a simple summary. Once everyone has seen it and the basic concept of the story is finalized, I start sketching it out. I pencil out the whole book and work hard to make sure everything is clear. Then I show it to my editors, and they read it through and ask me questions about it. If anything needs clarification, I rework pages and panels until we're all happy with it. After that, I start inking and ink the entire book at the rate of about two pages a day, and then, I show the book to everybody to get their feedback. I take all of their comments and suggestions into consideration and polish up the inks. The coloring process is the most time-intensive. I can really only color a page a day depending on the complexity. It's tough, but I'm also making small corrections along the way, and this is where the stories really come to life.

*What do you keep in mind for readers as you create?*

**Andy Runton:** I think it all comes down to trust. I truly believe that there is an understood contract between authors and readers. I'm asking them to join me on a journey, and they're trusting that I'll take care of them. Even though Owly sometimes gets sad and bad things and misunderstandings happen, I believe in happy endings, and I always make sure the whole experience is positive.

The flow of a story is also incredibly important. My background is in product design, and we have a saying, "If someone needs to read the directions to be able to use your product, it's a bad design." I try to make reading Owly stories effortless. If I did my job, there never needs to be an explanation and there should never be any question about what is happening.

*What drew you to comics?*

**Andy Runton:** Growing up, I always had trouble reading. I really still do. It never came easy for me. So, all of the amazing tales found in books were inaccessible to me. Comics were different. It's like it was made for my brain. My mom would read the funnies to me, and that's how I learned to read. The pictures said so much. I understood them and got lost in them. It took me a while to find comic books, but once I did, it was all I was interested in. I loved to draw and loved to create my own stories. I didn't think I could ever draw comics professionally, so I didn't pursue it for years. Once I did, it felt like coming home.

*What are your go-to sources for inspiration?*

**Andy Runton:** My love of animals, birds, and nature keeps me inspired. I love sitting outside and just observing all of the things going on and all of the details. There's so much wonder to see, and I try my best to capture a small sliver of it in my books. My source for artistic inspiration is my friends and colleagues. I love that everyone keeps trying to get better. For stories, I get inspiration everywhere. Even the smallest interaction can make me think about what Owly might do in that situation.

*What do you hope readers take away from your work?*

**Andy Runton:** I want them to see that kindness and understanding is a strength. It's sometimes really difficult, but it's the right thing.

*Any message for future teachers who might want to use comics?*

**Andy Runton:** When I grew up, only babies read books with pictures in them. As someone who was never diagnosed with anything and was in the gifted program, it destroyed me. Words didn't go in my mind the way they did for others. I was completely cut off from so much learning. All reading is reading; audiobooks, comics, graphic novels, picture books, magazines . . . it all counts.

If you're a teacher, I would ask that you see the visual medium of comics as a unique language. It's present in all aspects of our lives, from charts and graphs to street signs to product directions. Any student with visual literacy skills is better for it.

*Any message for the young creators they will work with?*
**Andy Runton:** I think frustration is the biggest enemy of anyone trying to learn how to create comics. A good comic looks effortless. Once you try to create even the most basic story, it's very easy to get overwhelmed. Start small. Don't worry about mistakes. Show your work to your friends, and see if they understand it. Maybe they have some ideas. Don't rewrite the same story over and over. Just move on and incorporate what you learn into the next one. You can do this! Owly and I believe in you.

# What's in a Word/World?
# Taking a Translinguistic Stance
# with Bilingual/Multilingual Comics

- *Learning for Justice—Identity Anchor Standard 1. Students will develop positive social identities based on their membership in multiple groups in society.*
- *Learning for Justice—Identity Anchor Standard 2. Students will develop language and historical and cultural knowledge that affirm and accurately describe their membership in multiple identity groups.*

In this chapter, I explore how learning takes place across bi-/multilingual and multimodal structures in classrooms as an aspect of critical literacy (Vasquez et al., 2019). In comics, I see the possibilities for language to occur alongside images with words occurring across and between a range of languages. Such work has the potential to showcase aspects of culture in invitational ways, positioning home language practices as both welcome in schools and as rich sources of knowledge (González et al., 2005). As one avenue of cultural exploration, I draw upon a translinguistic stance in this chapter and in my pedagogy (García et al., 2017). According to García, Lin, and May (2017), this stance is an "always dynamic set of practices for multilingual students experiencing the world and text through integrated linguistic system[s]" (p. 120). As a speaker of primarily one language, I note the beauty in a range of languages and linguistic practices, and I am drawn to books that use a variety of linguistic approaches. As Andy Runton hinted in the interview at the end of the last chapter, books with images offer much and can be a way of encountering language and culture in multidimensional and multimodal ways.

As is the case with memoir-based approaches to comics, the artifactual knowledge that children bring to class with them is not a matter to be left at home in favor of a monolingual or monolithic cultural space; rather, classrooms are ideally places where students and teachers are learning together. They are places in which children can bring their entire selves (including language) to be seen as aspects of their superpowers as readers and writers and as parts of their experiences to be celebrated. Scholars such as Sonia Nieto have reflected on the harmful practices of attempting to erase or contain children's cultures from public school spaces, subjecting students to a one-dimensional approach to languaging that diminishes practices outside of English. To stifle a child's languaging practice is to relegate their culture and way of being to a lesser-than or unwelcome sensibility—the opposite of the kind of environment we want to create as educators.

In my classroom practice, I have seen amazing possibilities in the connections that students make with comics across languages. In a high school classroom setting in late 2022, comics were the go-to texts for many of my students who were working toward being comfortable with English. One student created an example page, using images and Spanish.

Vasquez et al. (2019) note the possibilities for discussion that artifactual sharing can bring, and I see comics as the perfect avenue for sharing photos, words, and images from perspectives and lived experiences. Abraham and Kedley (2020) note, "Rather than enforcing a language policy or practice down onto people, a translanguaging theory of language is built up from the authentic language practices of people in their respective homes and communities" (p. 50). Abraham and Kedley (2020) advocate for an approach to language/literacy instruction that pulls down barriers and creates avenues of practice and communication for students. García et al. (2021) note the limited framing that educational policymakers use for academic and nonacademic language and the ways such approaches impose limitations on students who are bilingual, resulting in what they term "abyssal thinking" (p. 209). Simply put, there is no community that does not intersect with the life of the classroom, and the classroom is a representation of the life around it. This hive of linguistic and cultural activity is not a construct in which one view or way of being should be imposed; rather, the classroom is a collection of conversations that occur toward academic growth and deeper knowledge of the human experience.

Turning attention once more to comics, I highlight the work of Raúl the Third and the potential for including a perspective in reading visual texts that travels across words, images, and even the use of language. I especially note the potential in Raúl's Vamos and Lowriders series for bridging languages, quilting together words to create a classroom where cultures are honored and represented in written works. These titles work as a text set for readers from picture book stage to more developed comics, and the age group that is ideal for either textual type is a matter of flexibility.

## Traveling with Raúl the Third

When author and artist Raúl the Third suggests that readers "vamos," I am ready to travel along anytime based on my firsthand knowledge of this creator and his work. He has, in fact, been a guest in at least two virtual sessions I have been part of, and I have marveled as he has engaged with K–5 children in both English and Spanish. This journey with him started in the fall of 2020 when I was co-teaching with three other literacy scholars in an online reading clinic that invited children from our community and lab school academy. Raúl was a special guest that semester, and he returned later on to be an artist-in-residence.

My teaching team prepared for this experience by reading Raúl's picture book ¡Vamos! Let's Go to the Market (2019). The book features full-page spreads in a kind of ongoing textual journey that is based on a splash-page format with Spanish and English occurring side-by-side and in incidental print. By sharing a Kindle screen, I was able to navigate this world across digital devices with young children. Our class would pause often, taking in the smaller details of the images and inviting children to help us discover the meaning of Spanish words together. This was a learning experience for me both as a new way of teaching online and as an opportunity to revisit Spanish words (an immersion I had not engaged with since high school). Since then, I have also incorporated Raúl's graphic novel picture book series Tag Team in courses, as well as his co-created graphic novel series Lowriders (written by Cathy Camper). In each of these texts, language occurs in slightly different ways. In Tag Team books, English and Spanish appear side by side in complementary fashion, often providing an in-the-word-bubble translation, while in the Lowriders series, Spanish words are often explored further in footnotes. The response from my graduate students was positive with Lowriders; one student recounted how she had worked with a fourth grader who openly stated that he was not a reader, yet he engaged with Lowriders in its entirety, reading with her on a school field trip. Here again is a story that speaks to the power of these books.

An additional affordance that Raúl brings is his environmental and welcoming style. He not only centers creativity, comics, and culture, but he does so in a way that stems from his author and creator origins, picking up materials that were at hand to fashion developed and beautiful designs. His art looks as if it were drawn by a ballpoint pen, as these were readily available when he was coming of age, and the pages in his books sometimes resemble newsprint or notebook pages. Words appear in English and Spanish in the visual environment he constructs, working back and forth, to and fro, with no particular power dynamic in place to show one language over another.

Alongside this sensibility of organic and authentic creative practices that link up with Raúl's childhood artwork, the books also feature fanciful characters who navigate places like the mercado. Luchadores (professional wrestlers) are featured, and the images that Raúl construct have facets, details, and features that readers can spend long spans of time taking in with layer upon layer of content.

These are visual landscapes rich for exploring, and the Lowriders series uses not only language as a vehicle for literacy but the titular vehicle itself to navigate new lands, from space to the center of the earth.

In *El Toro & Friends: Tag Team* (2021), Raúl takes the reader into a picture book graphic-novel experience, or graphic picture book as Beth Frye has called it. The luchador character, El Toro, decorates the end pages, and the first spread is an invitation into the Coliseo setting with bold coloring by Elaine Bay. Throughout the book, Spanish appears alongside English translations, either as environmental print (as is the case with the Coliseo building) or in word bubbles. Toro, for example, speaks in English in black print and in Spanish in a different color. Separate word bubbles depict the languages in two different spaces set within the same print environment.

In the way he discloses his living and being in his work, Raúl exemplifies artistic and authorial, as well as cultural, invitation. I next feature an interview with *Lowriders* collaborator Cathy Camper before sharing lesson steps.

## Cathy Camper's Collaborative Process

*Please tell us about your creative process.*

**Cathy Camper:** People think writing starts on a computer or writing in a notebook, but for me, writing starts when I'm daydreaming, doing something kind of monotonous and boring like walking or doing the dishes. My body is occupied but my mind can daydream, think up new stories, or ask, "what if?" I also tend to get great ideas right when I wake up in the morning. I like to write down stories when I can start picturing them like a movie in my head.

*Please tell us about your collaborative process (thinking of Lowriders with Raúl the Third).*

**Cathy Camper:** When I thought up the story for *Lowriders in Space* and shared it with Raúl, he said, this is the story I wanted to read as a kid! And right away, he sent me pictures of the characters. We met through collaborating on zines, and just by luck we had a lot of things in common: our love of comics, our sense of humor, our sense of social justice, and our work ethic (if you want to get a book done, you have to meet deadlines and actually do the work!). For many kids' books, the author and illustrator work separately, and the editor does the communicating between them. But since Raúl and I submitted the book as collaborators, we've always talked about the ideas and worked as collaborators.

*What is your message for teachers and students about the value of comics in literacy?*
**Cathy Camper:** Adults often think that reading comics is "cheating" somehow and don't respect it as actually *reading*. But we live in an image-heavy world, and learning to read images is as crucial as reading text. Part of information literacy is also distinguishing the difference between what is written and what's in an image, and that can be a sophisticated skill. Also, for kids with ADHD, ESL students, and kids on the spectrum, pictures can help focus their reading, so it's good to always include some comics on kids' reading lists to give kids a choice to choose a book that is inviting to them.

## Classroom Application Ideas

When applying classroom practices to bi-/multilingual texts, I encourage teachers to think about approaches which build on inquiry-based knowledge of students, including aspects of culture and identity (Billen et al., 2022). Such approaches often look like a family culture night, but another way of linking to deep thinking and reflection in the classroom context can include allowing space for students to explore and share about their cultures through writing and responding. This process of giving students the opportunity to write and create across and between languages, using work in bi/multilingual texts as models, can support links between what is considered home and school practice, a relatively simplistic bimodal dynamic that has recently been the subject of debate. I encourage teachers to build on areas of interest, including popular characters, and to trace interests across languages and cultures using a variety of texts. I also encourage teachers to navigate the waters of multiple languages using assistance from co-teachers and community members who can act as translators as well as utilizing technology to build conversation across languages.

What's more, I encourage the use of words and images in mapping and body-mapping exercises (Lemieux et al., 2020), another creative direction that can include words or rely on images. Mapping and visualizing can be a way of exploring identity, experiences, and locations as well as a "spatializing activity focused on physical and social geography" (Lemieux et al., 2020, p. 3). According to these authors, such mapping can be done in both literal and figurative/metaphorical ways as students express their thinking and feelings. For mentor texts, I point back to the journey that is mapped across text in Shaun Tan's *The Arrival* (explored elsewhere in this book) and even the fun and lighthearted mapping in books like Remy Lai's *Pawcasso*, in which a pet's activities are explored from a cartoonish aerial view, and the picture book series, Scaredy Squirrel by Melanie Watt. Examples from this series take on a similar aerial view as the main character explores what is frightening and safe about the surrounding world. As already mentioned, the Vamos series makes beautiful use of maps and topographical excursions across spaces and ways of communicating.

Students can complete maps of school, maps of the first day of school, maps of a reading experience, and emotional and cognitive maps to visually depict their explorations. Again, the use of images provides a democratizing feature, as well as does the use of multiple languages for the purposes of explaining and labeling. Illustrating these experiences of places can help students share about experiences they find difficult as they navigate new places in addition to locating areas of commonality with their peers. Children can literally take teachers and peers on a visual and verbal tour of their worlds, highlighting the parts of their lives that are most important to them.

The use of multiple languages can be celebrated as part of the work. As with Abraham and Kedley's work (2020), these can be stories of travel, either accomplished or in transit and of both inward and outward journeys.

## Steps for Further Work (Including Additional Resources/Book Titles)

For additional reading and engagement, I recommend the collaborations between Minh Lê and Dan Santat, particularly the book *Drawn Together*. The book is a beautiful example of a picture book format merging with graphic novel design (or graphic picture book), and the use of the Vietnamese language exists without apology or translation.

I am drawn to these examples of texts that position language without the need to translate. Brian K. Vaughan, author of the adult-themed series Barrier (2018), has written about the ways that the images presented in comics allow for world-building and sharing story without the need to translate when languages other than English occur.

> *Where's Halmoni?* by Julie Kim (2017) has aspects of a traditional comics page, like word balloons, linking the book with the picture book format, along with comics grammatical features. The book features two young Korean American characters who enter a fantasy world of folklore. As with *Stargazing*, Korean linguistic characters are rendered on the pages, alongside English.

*Manu: A Graphic Novel* by Kelly Fernández (2021) is a story that features both Spanish and English and works as a middle grades novel incorporating supernatural elements and magical realism. For readers interested in using books that highlight dialects, like African American Vernacular English (AAVE), as natural parts of storytelling, I also recommend *Stuntboy, in the Meantime* by Jason Reynolds and Raúl the Third (2021).

Briefly broadening this chapter's scope, I also want to give a nod to the work of author and artist Gene Luen Yang (2020), who uses sports narrative as a historical example of how communities are brought together in his graphic novel *Dragon Hoops.*

In the absence of stories that feature the linguistic resources of all students, I recommend further creating with images and words across languages as classroom compositions, both in print and digital forms. This use of language can be daunting for teachers who are monolingual or who simply do not speak the languages of the students in their classrooms—being vulnerable and taking the spot of learner when it comes to language is a welcome pedagogical step in this process.

For older/young adult readers, I recommend the graphic novel *Himawari House* by Harmony Becker (2021) (see Figure 10.1). In Becker's work, a range of languages and dialects is showcased alongside English, and the experience of negotiating and navigating among languages is illustrated in this story of three young adults journeying through Tokyo. The book draws upon Becker's own experiences in travel and negotiating language.

I close this chapter with an interview with this author and artist.

## An Interview with Harmony Becker

*What inspires you to write?*
**Harmony Becker:** I think I'm always searching to articulate really specific ideas or feelings. I've always felt the most seen and connected while reading when an author expresses something that I've always felt but never quite had the words for.

*Please tell us about* Himawari House. *How did this book come to be?*
**Harmony Becker:** It started out as a webcomic that I was self-publishing on Tapas in 2017. Kiara Valdez, my editor, picked up my business card when we were

both at TCAF in 2018 (I did almost zero actual networking and still managed to get a book deal! It's an introvert's dream come true), and she reached out a couple of months later with an offer from First Second.

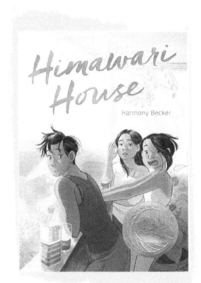

*How did you arrive at creating the characters that guide the narrative?*

**Harmony Becker:** I had a lot of sort of unrelated ideas that I wanted to write about, and I felt that assigning a theme/ story thread to each character was the best way to go about exploring all those ideas.

*What are the benefits and challenges of creating comics for the web?*

**Harmony Becker:** I really like the interactive element of webcomics—seeing people's comments as they got invested in the story was really encouraging. It's hard to answer this question without also taking into account the lifestyle I was leading at the time—

**FIGURE 10.1.** Image Courtesy of Harmony Becker

comics were a part-time thing for me, so I wasn't able to invest large chunks of time to it and was writing and drawing it as I went along. When I got the book deal, though, I was able to dedicate all my attention to the project, which really changed my approach.

*Please tell us about your writing and creating process.*

**Harmony Becker:** Like I just mentioned, the process changed a bit when *Himawari* got picked up as a graphic novel. In between that, I drew all of *They Called Us Enemy*, and I learned a lot that I then applied to *Himawari* when I came back to it—I started writing and working from a script, I transitioned to totally digital, things like that.

As far as coming up with the story went, I made a lot of preliminary sketches of the characters interacting, and I made a lot of notes of specific scenes I wanted to include or things I wanted to explore. The actual work comes in then, connecting all those things into a cohesive whole.

*What advice do you have for young comics makers?*

**Harmony Becker:** Don't wait until you're good enough for your own standards to start. Just start making work, and don't take yourself too seriously!

*What message do you want to send through your work?*

**Harmony Becker:** Ooh, that's a big question. In *Himawari House* specifically, there's a lot of messages, but if I were to pick one, I suppose it would be that you can create your own meaning in life and that you can find home, family, and joy anywhere.

*What is your author "origin story?"*
**Harmony Becker:** I was in my parents' garage a couple months ago and found a bunch of old comics and short stories we had made when we were kids, usually stories about our stuffed animals. When I got a little older and discovered manga, my sister and I would write and draw our own stories and leave a blank space every couple of pages for "reader Q&A." Those were a lot of fun.

*What was it like to collaborate with George Takei?*
**Harmony Becker:** I didn't actually work much with George directly, just when I would send in my work at several stages to get his feedback. I was really impressed by his dedication to his story, to making sure it lives on in the next generation. He also has a really sharp memory! He remembered so many details from places he hasn't seen since he was a little boy.

*What is the secret to a strong creative collaboration?*
**Harmony Becker:** I'm reevaluating this these days, as I'm thinking about the idea of approaching others for collaborating, which isn't something I've ever done before. I suppose I would say the most important thing is to have respect for your co-collaborators and to be flexible and humble.

# Comics Featuring Indigenous Peoples/First Nation Stories

I n this chapter, I explore stories of Indigenous peoples as presented in comics format in addition to global and community voices of place that are focused on bringing people together and celebrating both similarities and differences. Henzi (2016) has explored the ways that Indigenous peoples have been depicted in graphic novels and visual literature, including film, in stereotypical and demeaning ways. As students and teachers consider ways to act upon the world around them, it is important to note moments of limiting or problematic portrayals and recognize the aspects of history that have been amended or are not a centralized aspect of retellings of history. Drawing on the work of Paulo Freire, Carleton (2014) noted, "Freire's work firmly establishes that humans are both the products and potential changers of their lived circumstances" (p. 177).

When it comes to exploring books with this particular focus, educators can apply a number of steps for critique, including taking a close look at who is doing the authoring as well as the ways that notions of tribalism are portrayed and the ways that the customs of varied cultures are presented through a singular view. Many comics I have discovered draw upon the "Wild West" motif of good versus evil, oversimplifying the role of Native American/Indigenous cultures and reducing problematic moments in the history of American settlers. I also note that a number of books explore the mythological and legendary roots of Indigenous cultures and that there is more story to be told beyond these approaches. For example, the picture book/graphic novel *The Fox Wife* (2019) was a contender for the Excellence in Graphic Literature Award, and *Trickster: Native American Tales, A Graphic Collection* (2010) was a 2011 Eisner Award nominee and 2011 Aesop Prize winner.

These mythological/legend-based depictions can be seen as a potential area of reading and discussion, and educators can also expand viewpoints on Indigenous peoples beyond this framing. Such work can be done while noting additional authors who speak to community/communal experiences and stories of place. Also troubling is the low number of representations of Indigenous peoples in comics. M. L. Smoker, coauthor of the graphic novel *Thunderous* (2022), noted in an interview that "less than 1% of children's literature is by or about American

Indians, which is a very deplorable number" (n.p.). Chireau (2020) has also noted the tendency in comics to portray Indigenous peoples as ancillary members of white culture: "We see him with pink-tinged skin and azure eyes, as Manzar the Bright Arrow, thundering into battle on horseback in a feathered war bonnet" (p. 193).

There are multiple problematic layers in this kind of depiction, including the physical presentation of the character's skin color, but also the warrior/tribal trope that presents Indigenous peoples in extremely limited ways. Chireau pointed to the example of a 1950s character called the Apache Kid, "a comic about a white cowboy with a secret Native American crime-fighter alias" (p. 193). This narrative direction displaces "real indigenous presence by way of a complicated racial mimesis" (Chireau, 2020, p. 195).

## The Rez Detectives and Borders

*The Rez Detectives: Justice Served Cold* is a relatively brief graphic novel (60 pages), written by Steven Paul Judd and Tvli Jacob. The main character, Tasembo, encounters a mystery at hand in relatable experiences, and the book unfolds from there. M. K. Perker's artwork is colorful, attractive, and takes the reader into daily life on the reservation (the Rez) with richly drawn characters. Like the work mentioned in Chapter 10, *The Rez Detectives* features respectful and authentic representation of languages.

*The Rez Detectives* plays with mystery and has the potential to exist not only as a standalone story but as a series of ongoing mysteries. Life on the Rez is depicted in a way that is natural, organic, and authentic rather than as a quick glimpse into a surface level understanding of Indigenous/First Nations cultures in contemporary society. The presence of the mystery is a natural step in the story, and the Rez is not a token representation to serve as a unique foil or feature of the genre being explored.

The end pages of the book feature human and anthropomorphic characters with magnifying glasses and a footpath (complete with shoeprints). The central McGuffin, or missing piece of information in the narrative that becomes the focus of detection, appears on these pages as well as on the title page, creating opportunities for readers to make predictions about the coming narrative through visual cues. Upon opening up the first page, the reader is immediately transported to the "Sovereign Land of All Tribes" with the note that "Population Varies." The reader is told, "Welcome to the Rez" (n.p.). Aspects of culture, time, and place decorate each panel, as the reader notes "Indigenized Frozen Treats" with the tagline "THE FUTURE WILL BE INDIGENIZED" (n.p.).

A car is whisking by in the image as Redbone lyrics blare in the air (a potential link to the *Redbone* graphic novel for older readers and certainly a title to add to a reading playlist while engaging with the book). In an inset within the top panel, the main character welcomes us and begins to recount the story: "It was the first day of summer." The central problem of the hot days of summer is further established on the first page, with the threads of the narrative—characters, setting, and conflict—all being laid out for us within this connected series of panels.

As with other approaches to identities in text, I am on the lookout for authentic voices that present all people from a respectful and rounded perspective. Along with female, differently abled, and Black characters, depictions of Native/Indigenous/First Nations groups have a problematic history in comics.

For older students, I recommend *Borders* by Thomas King and Natasha Donovan (2021). The book tells the story of a family trip by a child and his mother from Alberta, Canada, to Salt Lake City. When confronted at the border with naming herself with a cultural/geographical identity that betrays her tribal affiliation, the mother refuses. This leads to a conflict between the family and the authorities with questions of place, identity, and property woven in. Through realistic artwork and well-paced visual narrative, King and Donovan present a family that finds themselves somewhere in the middle of space rather than having their cultural identity acknowledged, much less affirmed, by representatives of systems of power.

## Classroom Application Ideas

Questions from these books can be developed around the assumptions that students might have, as can the popular stories that are often told through media. Teachers can explore further historical nuances by expanding on what is often shared about Native/Indigenous stories. Teachers can also invite students to think about the importance of concepts like home and place and their cultures and customs that are regular parts of their lives in response to these texts. When an outside force attempts to impose a limitation on identity, what is the effect on a story, and how would this effect be felt in life? What is our responsibility for ensuring that stories are not erased?

Exploring these media presentations, including tropes of heroes and villains, is work that has been explored on film with young children (Tobin, 2000), including dress and manners of speech. Teachers can further follow up on these narratives with creative writing/designing activities. When creating in the classroom, even a stick figure representation can offer opportunities for exploring story; as McFarlane (2019) has noted, drawing "in general, benefits learning" (p. 48). While defining drawing "as a representation or look-alike of an object, character, or scene" (p. 48), McFarlane also notes, "Comics represent the unrepresentable" (p. 51).

All of this work leads to a critical approach to text that includes students as readers of the world around them and as composers of responses to the ideas they encounter. As Comber et al. (2018) noted, "Texts are constructed by the choices that text producers—speakers, writers, and designers—make when they compose a text" (p. 95). Teachers can work with students to think about the choices authors make when composing messages in both print- and image-based messages, including the biases and power structures that prioritize certain narratives or aspects of narratives. Texts are not magical objects that spring into being but are the result of intentional choices; the same is true for textbooks. We can critically examine the messages that we find, whether they occur in the context of social media or in the classroom. Historical and more recent treatments of Native/Indigenous peoples can be explored in this way, leading to opportunities to read and research more.

## Steps for Further Work (Including Additional Resources/Book Titles)

I recommend using the graphic novel informational text *A People's History of American Empire: The American Empire Project, A Graphic Adaptation* (2008). The book expands readers' knowledge about the simplified view of history rather than the broad strokes, and I contend that a full and honest view of history includes moments of struggle and failure in addition to heroic victories.

In fact, as I work with students to fashion a better world, honest conversations and mature, rounded views of historical events are paramount. This book was one of the first I encountered that provided details beyond the general historical narrative I encountered in school, and I wish I had engaged with a more fully developed understanding of this history from the ground up decades earlier. Learning about the historical colonization of North America and the forced removal of Indigenous/Native peoples was mentioned in my schooling but was hardly a major feature.

Duncan Tonatiuh is an author and artist whose work is collage-like and who presents Indigenous cultures through images and words. Tonatiuh was kind enough to engage in an interview, and his words conclude this chapter in addition to a view of his unique and wonderful artwork in Figure 11.1.

**FIGURE 11.1.** Image Courtesy of Duncan Tonatiuh

# An Interview with Duncan Tonatiuh

*What is your creative process?*

**Duncan Tonatiuh:** I was definitely inspired by superhero comics as a kid. That was one of the reasons why I started drawing. My cousins and I were really into Spider-Man and the X-Men, and we often drew our own superheroes and supervillains. We would get together over summer breaks and make our own comics. That's always been an interest of mine.

I grew up in Mexico, but then I came to the US when I was about fifteen years old. I have family in both countries. I began to miss things that were around me growing up, like the music, food, and traditions. I became more interested in the art and the culture of Mexico. Sometimes, when you're surrounded by things, you don't think much about them. But when you are away, you notice them. The Day of the Dead, for example, is pretty unique and special, but I didn't realize that until I lived somewhere where the holiday wasn't celebrated as much.

I went to art school in New York City. I was able to take a lot of writing classes, too. My last year, I had to have a senior project, and I wanted to do something that involved drawing and writing. I was very inspired by graphic novels at the time, like *Maus* and *Persepolis,* and I wanted to do something that talked about politics or about current events. I had taken a class called "Community Organizing," and because of it, I met a Mixtec friend named Sergio at a worker center. Mixtecs are an Indigenous group from southern Mexico. Sergio had fought for better wages and working conditions at a restaurant where he worked even though he was undocumented. His story inspired my senior project.

Soon after I began working on my thesis, I went to my university's library and looked up Mixtec artwork. I found Mixtec drawings in books. There are modern-day Mixtecs, but the Mixtecs were also a civilization that lived hundreds of years ago. They made books, which we now call codices. The books they made were painted on the hides of deer. They were long strips that could be folded accordion-style. Mixtec art is very stylized, flat and geometric. Everyone is drawn in profile. I was inspired by Mixtec artwork for my project. I began drawing in a similar style, but I also began to collage a lot of textures and pictures into my illustrations. That is why some parts of my drawings look very realistic.

In the middle of the semester while my classmates and I were working on our projects, we had to show our work to professors from the university. A teacher thought that what I was doing was very interesting and showed my drawings to an editor that she was friends with. The editor thought that my project was interesting, but it was too adult; he focused on books for younger readers. I told him I liked writing and that perhaps I could write a picture book for him. That meeting eventually led to my first published book.

*What are the stories that are not told enough in comics?*
**Duncan Tonatiuh:** When I was in college, I often tied the assignments I had to my Mexican background. I remember I took a photography class, and for my assignment, I decided to go photograph a march in which a lot of Mexican immigrants were protesting. I also remember taking a writing class and writing a short story that was set in San Miguel, trying to remember what it was like when I was a kid. Doing those assignments was a way for me to connect with my Mexican culture. It was a way to celebrate it, remember it, and discover more about it.

After I started making books for young readers, I became familiar with the publishing industry, and I became aware of the need for more diversity. In the US, there are thousands of books that are published for young readers every year, but only a very small percentage of them are about Mexican American, Latino/a, Asian American, Native, or African American children. Even though the United States is a very diverse country and there are so many different backgrounds that kids have, the books that are available don't really reflect that diversity. I think it's important for children to see themselves in books.

For me, one example of the power of books and representation came after I made *Pancho Rabbit and the Coyote*. The book is a fable with animals that talk, but it is also an allegory of the journey and dangers that migrants often go through to reach the US Soon after the book came out, I was at a book festival, and I was introduced by a group of students. They shared with the audience a video of a multi-voice poem that they wrote after reading my book. The poem was about their own border-crossing experiences. I was very moved by their stories, and I felt that my book helped them know that their experiences and their voices are important.

Kids need to see their experiences, culture, and traditions reflected in books. The diversity in the United States is what makes the country special. You can be proud that your family comes from another country, be proud of your language, food, and traditions, and be a good member of the US. All of that diversity adds to the country. Books can be a way to showcase that variety, and books can be a way to learn about someone else. People sometimes speak of books as mirrors where you can see yourself and your community and also as windows where you can learn about someone else. That makes complete sense to me.

*What do you think about the place of comics for reading and readers?*
**Duncan Tonatiuh:** I was very motivated to read, draw, and write because of comics. I think they are [a] very engaging medium. I have young children, and my daughter is really into them.

Comics can seem simple, but they are a very sophisticated art form. They have their own rules and logic. Comics are very entertaining, and they can be super-informative. They can be a wonderful way to acquire language and learn about different themes. I remember reading one of *Nathan Hale's Hazardous Tales* when I was doing research for one of my books and trying to learn more about World War I.

*What is the message you want to share through your work?*
**Duncan Tonatiuh:** There are several messages. One broad message in my books is the importance of multicultural literature. Other messages depend on each book. There are different topics that I am passionate about. I'm very interested in social justice and in telling stories of unsung heroes. I'm interested in art, and I've made several books about artists that I find interesting. Mythology is also something that I enjoy, and I've done a few books that deal with the pre-Columbian mythology and legends. I feel very lucky that I am an author and illustrator. I get to learn about subjects that I care about. I then try to distill what I learned and present it in a picture book format.

All of my books so far have to do with Mexican culture or Mexican American culture in some way. It is something that I care about and that hopefully I can speak about in an authentic way. My books often have an educational message. I try not to be too didactic. Hopefully, students infer the messages and the themes of my books. I want students to feel reaffirmed about who they are and learn more. I am fulfilled when I see students responding to my work.

One thing that I need to mention is that it is a challenging time to be an author and illustrator due to the banning of books that is happening across the country. It's very frustrating, and I think they are totally politically motivated. I think it's terrible to attack books that deal with race and gender and to make it challenging for people to use them in the classroom. It's a great disservice to ban those books because there is already such a limited number of them. It's fair for people to not like a book or to criticize it; if you don't like a book, don't read it. But it's a great disservice to prohibit others from reading them and accessing them. I disagree entirely with banning books.

# Broadening Windows of Text through Additional Applications

# Explorations of Mental Health and Grief in Graphic Novels

- *Learning for Justice—Identity Anchor Standard 3. Students will recognize that people's multiple identities interact and create unique and complex individuals.*
- *Learning for Justice—Diversity Anchor Standard 9. Students will respond to diversity by building empathy, respect, understanding and connection.*

While grief, trauma, and issues related to mental health are quite common, they also continue to be stigmatized in our society. Part of the work of advocacy I engage in as an educator is the willingness to say (a) I've been there, or (b) I've been in similar places or am just as likely to have similar struggles. As is so often stated, each of us has burdens to carry, and we do so in particular ways, and we all need help at times in our lives. I note this truth as someone who has processed rejection and even long-term trauma and as someone who has experienced the anticipatory grief caused by a global pandemic. I also note that there are experiences that I do not have full-fledged insights into and that there are many times I take on the role of listener. Without this step toward compassion, classrooms are much more difficult places to be, regardless of the texts that are being explored.

The work of storytelling takes me to uncomfortable places where I must admit my humanness and recognize my limitations. Even a simple statement like "I don't know" is a step in a positive direction when encountered with an experience or challenge that I have not yet thought about. In the model shared by Vasquez et al. (2019), educators can note that students engage with work that links to their experiences in relevant ways. Just as Vasquez et al. suggested that texts are not neutral in terms of sociopolitical issues and questions, texts also tackle complex topics of lived experience, including moments of grief and trauma. Sometimes, my middle grades students would ask about the recurring moments of death or loss that were part of the stories we read as a class. It was certainly not part of the reason why I selected these texts, but I was quick to explain to students that literature is often written to explore difficult questions. Death, loss, and grief are certainly some of the difficult aspects of life we encounter as humans.

Talking about topics like this may not be the most comfortable lesson steps. Helpfully, books take us there. Uncomfortable conversations are made accessible by books like *When Stars Are Scattered*, in which traumatic events shape characters and topics like parent loss and separation can be examined. Indeed, I see books as inviting vehicles for difficult conversations in the classroom (Husbye et al., 2019). Books make such difficult discussions possible, and they offer places to look to know that readers are not alone. Savitz and Stockwell (2021) have noted the power of student voices in both witness and testimony when in moments of trauma and grief. As playwright William Nicholson noted in his 1989 work, *Shadowlands*, part of engaging with reading is this linking to others so that readers (students) know that they are part of a larger story and network of experiences.

In this chapter, I highlight graphic novel texts that allow for processing mental health/wellness and grief. As I have mentioned *Stargazing* in a previous chapter, I spend less time on it here in favor of exploring both *Guts* by Raina Telgemeier (2019) and *Pilu of the Woods* by Mae K. Nguyen (2019). Comics have been explored as sites of processing difficult experiences through bibliotherapy (the use of texts to process complicated experiences) with upper elementary children (Schoonover et al., 2021) as well as with older readers in grades 6–12 (Gavigan, 2012). Bibliotherapy has been practiced with children, even at young ages, for some time (Pardek, 1990; Prater et al., 2006; Rozalski et al., 2010).

There are many ways of experiencing trauma, grief, and concerns of mental health. The goal of being both a critical and compassionate educator is supported by the work of normalizing and extending moments of listening through texts rather than glossing over questions through a deceptively simple structure or lesson design. I would not offer a single, simplified pamphlet for all of the challenges that one might encounter in working with readers. Sometimes authors and artists provide visual and textual links to common journeys with students that I am not even aware of.

## Deep Forests of Meaning

Books for children, including comics and graphic novels, can be rich sources of lived experience and exploration, using deceptively simple arrangements of words and images in often magical and engaging ways. This is part of the complexity and beautiful nature of children's literature. Just as *The Witch Boy* by Mollie Knox Ostertag (discussed in Chapter 6) deals with gender roles in society within a fanciful conceit, *Pilu of the Woods* deals with loss and grief, drawing upon fantasy elements. In addition to the graphic novel-based presentation of the text, *Pilu* includes a recipe and nature journal in the back of the book. This is both an invitation to read and to write and is part of the wonderful work that creators sometimes include in the additional materials readers can encounter together in the classroom.

Shaded panels provide comprehension work around the narrative with flashbacks, providing questioning opportunities about plot development, timelines, and potential reasons why characters may be responding in the ways they do. Readers must interpret these visual designs, as they do with *Robot Dreams*, to grasp the flow of the narrative. I am again thinking of the powerful of sticky note annotations to mark shifts in the text or record thoughts, including predictions and inferences. In elegant terms, the book explores the main character's relationship with her mother and confronts the topic of loss. Notably, the conversation around loss takes place in a mythical forest and in conversation with a fantastical foil character, Pilu. This setting and approach make for an accessible and imaginative exploration of both the story and central themes. With the visual narrative, the reader can see the ideas that are swirling in the mind of the main character, Willow. Panel 20B, for example, includes both hovering language like "GROW UP A LITTLE!" and "OUT OF CONTROL!" while an inset panel (20Ba) features Willow's tearful face and emotional expression. These are powerful and sometimes difficult emotions to explore that stem from events in life that young children (and even adults) sometimes lack the coping skills to deal with. This is why the fantasy presentation in the book is so palatable, making the very challenging parts of life approachable and crafting visual/creative and imaginative invitations to further conversation and even personal storytelling through a variety of means. While some readers may gravitate toward fantasy, I note the limitations that genres sometimes bring with them. I also note that there are levels and layers of grief that can be touched on but not adequately dealt with in a singular approach. The book is meant to be an introduction and brief exploration of one dimension/experience of grief while a number of other experiences may only be glimpsed. The back-and-forth nature of the narrative unfolds the story for the reader rather than supplying all information directly at the beginning, and the fanciful aspects of the story add to this sense of making the uncomfortable more inviting. It is a kind of collective understanding that can be co-constructed between teacher, student, and author/illustrator throughout the reading process.

Exploring issues related to mental health expands well beyond grief, and children bring stories with them to class each day in the form of what they are experiencing at home. I recommend open and rich conversations with school counselors, as well as with families, and I also note that teachers have much on their plates with state standards, curricular demands, and other factors, and are not licensed therapists. Aligning myself with the message of Raina Telgemeier's

*Guts*, utilizing the assistance and expertise of a therapist is a mark of strength rather than of weakness, and it is one that I and loved ones and friends in my life have drawn upon as a reservoir of processing and understanding. Such experiences and resources, at times seen as somehow secretive or shameful, can be powerful as we become better humans.

Following from the phenomenological work of scholars Mandie Dunn and Antero Garcia, I am reminded that teachers themselves experience grief and need mental health support. Though we are leaders as educators, we are also humans with needs, vulnerabilities, and our own truths and experiences to process. As leaders, we must also take time to ensure that we have healthy boundaries and that we are doing what is best for our well-being and the well-being of those whom we love.

## Texts That Don't Quite Fit

I recommend that as teachers curate books in their classroom libraries related to mental health and grief, they consider the prevalence of both the stigma of and sympathy given to these topics. Authentic, engaged empathy is required, beyond the temptation of performative hyper-awareness, and this is delicate work. It is too easy to take on the role of rescuer; teachers guide students and engage with community resources that are more equipped for helping process trauma and grief. There is a difference between showcasing pity and, much preferably, giving ourselves and our students grace and permission to be human. As Mandie Dunn noted in her dissertation work, not all teachers feel they have room or permission to grieve.

With the many demands that I have alluded to, I wish to again return to this notion of a network and community of support, including conversation with school counselors and awareness of organizations and resources in the community, for helping children deal with difficult experiences. Educators can consider questions such as

- In the midst of curriculum, do I make time to check in with my needs?
- In the midst of curriculum, do my administrators take time to check in with me?
- With all of the demands of my job, how do I center the health and well-being of my students?
- In what ways do the texts in my classroom showcase a range of experiences—and what kinds of experiences do I need to add reflections for in my book collection?

Texts that skim the surface or deal with traumatic events in an overly simplistic fashion may be considered, but additional conversation and work might be done as teachers consider texts that speak to and add to these topics. I attempt to engage in the work of encouraging students to process experiences, as is the case in Figure 12.1, composed in the context of a very busy and packed semester after the student/intern had just completed time in classrooms.

Linking to the visual, teachers can make time for social and emotional check-ins with students to gauge their feelings, and teachers can invite students to consider their areas of strength and purpose using words and pictures. What, in effect, are the superpowers that students bring with them to the classroom? While coloring is an aspect of comics pages that is not always analyzed as closely as images, coloration can hold potential for discussing the emotional impact of pages. Notice instances where the use of red denotes anger or passion, where blue indicates a sense of calm, or where green indicates growth. Even the verdant setting of *Pilu of the Woods* can indicate this sense of dense and lost forest as well as the sense of growth that Willow explores. The main character's organic

**FIGURE 12.1.** Teacher-Created Illustration of Crafting Plot in Comics

and herpetological namesake offers opportunities for further conversation. The contrasts of light and dark (graphic weight) can sometimes carry emotions, as can the coloration that occurs outside of the panels themselves. In Ostertag's *The Witch Boy* (2017), pages appear in a light shade when the narrative is proceeding without major conflict, but when the primary antagonist of the book is introduced, the pages are rendered in an inky darkness. Baetens (2011) has also examined the use of color in comics.

## Classroom Application Ideas

While I hesitate to ask students to share personal information, I do see great opportunities in noting characters that exist in texts and discussing ways that characters deal with challenges. Journaling is another powerful avenue of processing and potential sharing as well. The traditional plot diagram comes to mind here when thinking about a story's overarching development, but there are additional possibilities for thinking about a close look at a character's "mountain climb" in a text, including the ways they have overcome and the resources they use to find a place of healing and ultimately helping others. This is the hero's journey, and it is one that can be traced across a mountain-like graphic organizer, inspired by Joseph Campbell's work on the archetypes that can be found in stories. (I recommend his book *Hero with a Thousand Faces* for more information about these archetypes.) Students can be invited to share their own "mountain climb" stories—as a way of inviting the conversation, teachers can focus the tracing of journey and overcoming difficulties, including mental health challenges and grief, on the work that characters go through. Perhaps by seeing characters navigate setbacks and process emotions in narrative form, young readers can begin to feel less alone. From these reading experiences, students may wish to share their own ideas and experiences.

Additionally, the emotional expression found in visual representation (see again Panel 20Ba) provides opportunities for teachers to discuss and unpack emotions. I suggest that readers in our classrooms have spaces where they can go to process emotions through words and images, and often I do so poetically in both my personal and professional practice. These spaces can be print-based reader's/writer's notebooks or digital spaces for processing. This work is inspired by Dutro's (2011) treatment of writing through wounds on both the part of the student and teacher. I further encourage teachers to think through carefully which aspects of their experiences and vulnerability to share with students in critical spaces where children are given time and opportunities to think through events. As mentioned in earlier chapters, our stories are part of our power, and we decide what and when to share.

I recognize that both teachers and students have moments of hurt and trauma that require time and space (Dunn, 2021). A prompt might be shared along the lines: "Create a quick sketch or comics panel to show how you feel after reading" or "Create an image that shows how you believe the author wants you to feel." These prompts can then be followed up on with opportunities to take close looks at character actions and words, as well as the descriptions and word choices of authors, to create these emotional experiences. As is the case with visual texts, the choices authors and artists make in visual representations provide yet more room for discussion and processing.

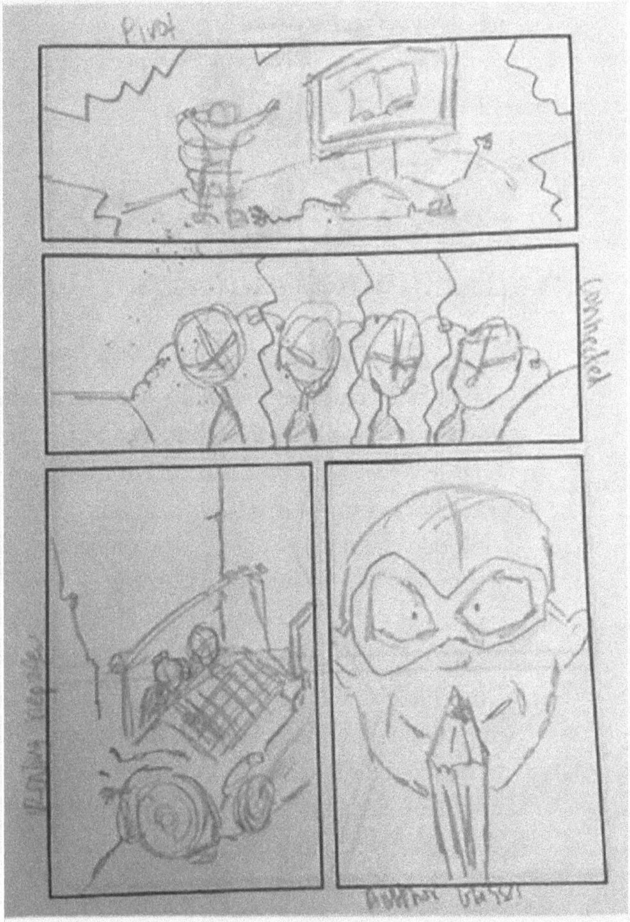

Teachers can also work with students in lessons centered on mood and tone to discuss emotions and then ask students to respond with pictures and symbols that they

**FIGURE 12.2.** Author Explores the Pandemic Experience through Comics Creation

feel might represent a particular emotion (e.g., anger, sadness, hope) in a narrative or in general.

In the private spaces of journals, through words and images, it is my hope that students can begin to process events in ways that are healthy and fulfilling. I again suggest that teachers are made keenly aware of the resources that are afforded within their schools and communities for students who have deep and resonant needs. Taking the time to artistically represent an experience, like the shifts that occurred in the COVID-19 pandemic (pictured in Figure 12.2), provides a space for recounting and taking stock of moments in life that we sometimes miss in our busy rush to the next item on our agenda or pacing guide. The images capture the feeling of a sudden pivot in what was natural, comfortable, and expected, as well as the feelings of disconnect followed by the human interaction I was able to experience in online instructional settings. I have found both poetry and visuals helpful in processing parts of life in addition to thinking in my research.

## Steps for Further Work (Including Additional Resources/Book Titles)

*The Aquanaut* by Dan Santat is an example of the ever-growing corpus of comics available for reading instruction. Santat has been noted as a collaborator in texts I have mentioned in other chapters, but he is here both author and artist.

While this book was not part of my original plan for this chapter, it has been published as this current writing has come to be. In Santat's (2022) words, the book became a story about loss, preserving legacies, family, and holding on to memories, "which began with the idea of sea creatures attempting to use a diving suit to live among land-dwellers" (p. 46).

As an additional graphic novel option, teachers might consider exploring *Better Place* by Duane Murray and Shawn Daley (2021). *Better Place* features a grandchild/grandfather relationship and uses superhero storytelling as a way for the young main character to deal with the knowledge that his grandfather has moved on to a "better place." The work is beautifully rendered and emotionally resonant, showcasing a familial relationship alongside the tropes of what one might consider a typical superhero comic.

In *Stuntboy, in the Meantime,* author Jason Reynolds and artist Raúl the Third (2021) share the story of "Stuntboy," the superheroic alter-ego of the main character, Portico Reeves. Stuntboy is an invention for dealing with trauma and emotion, including divorce. In a 2021 interview on *Late Night with Stephen Colbert,* Jason Reynolds pointed to the prevalence and widespread nature of trauma, especially in the midst of the pandemic and continuing racial disparity. In *Stuntboy,* the reader has a comics-based representation of dealing with the realities of life, even from a young age. The book resembles an illustrated chapter book at times while also drawing upon more direct comics conventions in key places.

For older readers, I recommend Jason Walz's 2013 autobiographical graphic memoir *Homesick*. This emotional book works as a visual memoir that can be used to encourage personal writing. While the genre work of Walz's *Last Pick* is not a focal point in this book, *Homesick* is a powerful personal reflection (see

Chapter 7 for an interview with Walz, plus additional conversation with him at the end of this chapter).

*Small Things* by Mel Tregonning (2018) wordlessly illustrates childhood experiences of tension and anxiety. The black-and-white art is striking, and readers can journey through the images with the questioning and affirming guidance of a teacher who can help them unpack the images and discuss their own connections in a safe space. Tregonning takes the feelings of worry that the young protagonist feels in *Small Things* and fashions them visually as small creatures that trouble him. This is the perfect example of how a comics text can use images to convey an idea or experience that can only otherwise be expressed with a limited set of words—"worried" can mean so many things.

As hinted earlier in this chapter, this choice of absence of color is visually striking and creates a powerful emotional effect. The book was the 2018 Foreword INDIES: Graphic Novels & Comics Bronze Winner, was a 2019 USBBY Outstanding International Books List selection, and was on the 2019 Pop Culture Classroom Excellence in Graphic Literature Awards: Best in Children's Graphic Literature shortlist.

Finally, I once more recommend *Guts* by Raina Telgemeier. A key scene in this book normalized therapy and emotional processing, linking with the emphasis I have attempted to place on seeking support systems, and the emotional working through of the author/artist is a central narrative point. Telgemeier has done much to expand the graphic novel form by fashioning attractively designed texts that feature young characters dealing with real-life issues, often related to the author/artist's own experiences. Telgemeier is one of the major figures in positioning comics as classroom reading. Notably, Telgemeier has also been the target of book bans as political groups have sought to censor access to visual representations of LGBTQ+ youth. As noted throughout this text, it is essential that readers have access to books. While parents can determine what they want their children to read, this should never mean that one family or even set of families should determine what is acceptable for everyone.

The work of recognizing that everyone needs a community of friends and family to support us and that no one embarks on this journey alone is a powerful aspect of this story, as is the visual depiction of the notion that even the comics creators whose works are featured at the school book fair have gone through experiences and continue to process emotions about the world around them. Human beings, indeed, read to know that there are others in the world who can link to our experiences in one way or another. Books nurture, help us know we are not alone, and help us learn about experiences that might help us empathize with and embrace our fellow humans. Graphic novels and comics are not a set of "bonus features" or candy books but instead are powerful artistic works that show and tell parts of life.

# Notes on *Homesick* by Jason Walz

*In addition to the* Last Pick *series, I know you have also written and illustrated books called* A Story for Desmond *and* Homesick.

**Jason Walz**: You've done a deep dive. *A Story for Desmond* is a small mini-comic that you have to special order. *Homesick* was about losing my mom to cancer; *A Story for Desmond* was about trying to find the positives in that experience—not that there's really anything positive about that part of my life. But this book was about passing on some stories to her grandchildren. I wanted to put a spin on it that wasn't so dark, and hopefully that could show some hope in all of that.

*So, the first couple of books you did were autobiographical. It's that idea of writing through experiences, including the pandemic.*

**Jason Walz:** Yeah, getting through a pandemic. I just had COVID for the second time. I am vaccinated. It feels like the never-ending story. It's such a cliché, but "write what you know" is extremely important and valid. We are all experiencing some trauma that we can all relate to, and getting it on paper is pretty powerful. Same with *Homesick*. I've been making comics my whole life but never with the thought of getting them out into the world. When my mom died, I had a lot on my mind, and that kind of grief was specific to me but universal to everybody in some way or another. I felt passionate that this was a story that I could tell and needed to tell. I've had people read my books and tie them to other experiences, and I'm thinking, "Well, I guess that's in there, too."

# Texts of Freedom/
# Texts of Great Power
# and Great Responsibility

- *Learning for Justice—Justice Anchor Standard 14. Students will recognize that power and privilege influence relationships on interpersonal, intergroup, and institutional levels and consider how they have been affected by those dynamics.*
- *Learning for Justice—Action Anchor Standard 17. Students will recognize their own responsibility to stand up to exclusion, prejudice, and injustice.*

While it is one thing to read books in which others note problems in the world around them and work to make change, there are additional possibilities for engaging with students in this work. As Vasquez, Janks, and Comber (2019) note, "Critical literacy practices can be transformative" (p. 307). While powerful work can be done with changing minds in the classroom, the work of critical literacy and engaging with sociopolitical realities around us does not stop at the classroom door. With this frame in mind, texts do not exist as ends in themselves, but they transform the reader and enable wider transformation of intellect and culture.

## Themes Across Works

As we have explored graphic novels and comics together throughout this book, we have seen a number of common themes. What draws us to comics? For me, it was the story of a hero who could introduce me to a new way of reading and writing—but also a new way of being. The visual elements of comics allowed for engagement with pages well before I, as a young reader, knew how to tackle all of the words on the page. Over and over again, these pages could be encountered and offer something new, like the lyrics of a well-played song. Were they only about superheroes, comics could only do so much. Throughout these chapters, however, I have presented and explored stories of voices that have been silenced or sidelined, and I have provided examples to think about the possibilities of what the comics medium can offer us for storytelling, both for readers along for the ride and as writers who are fashioning the next steps.

There is a thematic sense of hope in many comics, an agency for characters, and a visual representation of a world that can be improved upon. There is certainly the superhero story that can be considered, but there are also stories of triumph, as when characters come together across challenging circumstances that build understanding and empathy (see Jen Wang's *Stargazing*) or when characters embrace their identity and begin to see the beauty in themselves (see Claribel A. Ortega and Rose Bousamra's *Frizzy*) or when characters confront the inequities and issues around them by speaking up and finding their voices (see Jerry Craft's *New Kid*).

Building on a content area perspective, graphic novels have become sites for political pushback and social discussion in addition to action around ecological issues (see Jonathan Case's *Little Monarchs*). I further note that we live and teach in times of tension, and teachers and students can view graphic novels as textual spaces for expressing some of these feelings through a variety of print and digital (and hybridized) composing practices. Comics can be a kind of artivism, a linking of art and activism in which the methods and tools of artistic craft can be drawn upon for a social justice-oriented message to begin to work on making changes in the world around us. In short, critical literacy is transformational work, and comics are perfectly positioned to not only tell but show the inequities in the world around us.

## Taking Action

For younger readers, teachers can highlight *Act* by Kayla Miller (2020) as an accessible chapter book/graphic novel that focuses on the changes that young people can make in the world around them as activists and artivists. I might again use the word *transitional* here not to suggest that this book is on its way to being a "real book" but that the book exists somewhere between modalities of graphic novel and the design of a chapter book. In the book, Olive, the main character, notices something in the world around her that she wants to change and begins to take action. The book is excellent for highlighting the ways young children can begin to practice advocacy and engagement in their world in meaningful steps. Sometimes the problems of the world seem insurmountable and, even as adults, it seems that there is little we can do—yet *Act* reminds us that even small steps forward count as progress and that our voices can be heard.

Author/artist Miller dedicates the book with the message, "For all the troublemakers and problem solvers," and sets up the relationships in the book from the very beginning. Before diving into a social message, which could come across as superficial, inauthentic, or didactic, Miller positions relationships and characters first and then allows the central conflict to evolve from there as the panels unfold.

*Act* also includes interdisciplinary possibilities, set in the early stages of the narrative, in which the main character and her friends are given a lesson in social studies in their classroom, including aspects of democracy. Again, this part of the story feels organic and woven in as an inspiration for and foreshadowing of what will come later. Through the panels on page six, the reader encounters working knowledge of democracy, including a peek inside Olive's notebook, explaining the inner workings of a direct democracy in a comics-afforded graphic organizer. While informational, this comes across as classroom notes from the character and not as a textbook-like feature. On the next page, Olive affords us a comparison of direct and representative democracy.

I note the use of the visual and the invitational nature of Miller's style. These are complex ideas packed tightly and neatly into interactions among characters and graphic elements that feel natural in this story. Within the space of a graphic novel, the reader can enjoy a brief lesson in social studies—without pausing the storyline to take a jarring sidestep. The content is not presented didactically but unfolds as part of the story structure. This kind of inclusion of informational detail is also seen in Case's *Little Monarchs* with a narrative structure meeting moments in the text that almost resemble text features found in science texts.

For older readers, teachers might consider the work of Nate Powell as an additional stretch text. Once again using fantastical/animal characters, Powell depicts himself accurately in his 2021 book *Save It for Later* while depicting his children fantastically. This is the effect of magic entering the narrative and of childhood and innocence exploring the rocky terrain of the pandemic Trump-era context. Notably, these political topics have been polarizing in society, and the book can be a source of perspective-building. In one key scene, Powell explores the decision to march or not to march, an ironic exchange for the artist behind the book series *March*, and navigates this experience for the reader. In another scene, Powell showcases the experience of going to the grocery store in the early days of the pandemic—a simple daily routine that was disrupted and changed by the context.

## What's Missing?

In the graphic novel adaptation of his 2021 book *What Unites Us*, author Dan Rather muses on the definition of a patriot, and he reconfigures this word not as one who must love their country regardless of its history and current wrongs but as one who loves their country so much that they desperately want to see it improved upon. While there is pride and privilege in being American citizens, thoughtful citizens can also note that there is work to be done. Rather's work, adapted into comics form, reinforces this notion and is one of several titles published in First Second's World Citizen Comics series.

Educators can be grateful for brave authors and artists who call attention to the ways the world still needs changing, and readers can build a collective sense of awe for current and future students who are taking up this work as change agents. Helping students see themselves as active voices, and even activists, is part of culture-transforming literacy practice, and it is an aspect of digital citizenship that extends beyond the series of boundaries that are usually part of instruction around this topic (Buchholz et al., 2020).

## Visual Advocacy Projects

As hinted above, educators can encourage students to explore social media and visual formats for making change. Young people have an increasingly wide audience, given the platforms that are now available to them. While this access to the world is often viewed through a negative light, I see great potential in encouraging youth to be activists and to inspire social change in positive ways through access to technology.

Educators can help students recognize the agentive power that is contained in popular characters like Spider-Man in the world of comics, with a focus on both power and responsibility, and I encourage teachers to expose young readers to graphic novel narratives that both include and expand the superhero genre. As a starting point, teachers can pose questions like: What makes a hero? What positive qualities do I have? What are the needs in my community?

From there, teachers can work with students to craft their individual and classroom community maps or codes, and they can talk about positive action that can be accomplished through art, including the nature and history of propaganda (Hobbs, 2020). I include an example of my work in this in Figure 13.1. Classrooms are community-building work, and teachers can connect to the mission and vision of schools and districts to meaningfully unpack what it means to be a thoughtful citizen and a member of the wider community.

I crafted the image shown in Figure 13.1 to develop "code work" around ways that students and teachers could begin to think about social action and their decisions in digital environments—but this is only one example of the kind of collective thinking that teachers can lead students in.

## Steps for Further Work (Including Additional Resources/ Book Titles)

In addition to the titles that have been highlighted in this chapter, I recommend the March trilogy, co-written by the late Congressman John Lewis and Andrew Aydin and illustrated by Nate Powell. The narrative is hard-hitting and based on Lewis's own steps in making "good trouble" as a youth and his experiences encountering racism and tension in the world around him. Powell continued the narrative in the 2021 graphic novel *Run*.

Additionally, teachers might consider using books like *Displacement* by Kiku Hughes (2020) and *They Called Us Enemy* by George Takei (featuring Harmony Becker's work) (2019) as books that can help young readers learn about the problematic history of Japanese internment camps. Hughes takes on

**FIGURE 13.1.** A Visual Demonstration of Classroom Building with Jordan from New Kid

a fantasy conceit to carry her main character back and forth through time to encounter the realities of this time while Takei tells his own story in more realistic ways. Hughes also renders political figures in the narrative in ways that form a visual sociopolitical critique.

Finally, I would remiss if I did mention *Maus* by Art Spiegelman (1986), a book that was challenged in a Tennessee school district in early 2022 and on other occasions before then. As a teacher who has taught about this time period, I advocate strongly for the telling and retelling of this story, which uses cats and mice in an anthropomorphic fable of the Holocaust. I further point to *White Bird: A Wonder Story* by R. J. Palacio (2019) and *Hidden: A Child's Story of the Holocaust* by Loïc Dauvillier (2014) as graphic novels that focus on the Holocaust. I further recommend the allegory *Terrible Things* by Eve Bunting (1980), which is a picture book—but quite complex and evocative.

The stories we tell and retell will be remembered, and it is vital work on the part of teachers and librarians to continue sharing these stories, even as forces in the world around us push back and attempt to silence history.

As a conclusion to this chapter, I include words from writer and artist Jared Cullum, whose book *Kodi* features themes of friendship and communing with nature.

## Words from Jared Cullum

*Please tell us your author "origin story."*

**Jared Cullum:** I have always had an interest in art and drawing but like many people was discouraged at a certain point for practical reasons. I was always interested in animation and storytelling, although I did not get into comics until I was in my mid-20s when a friend introduced me to the book Blankets. At the time, my mind was completely blown. I had quit drawing around sixteen because I felt like (and was told by well-meaning mentors at the time) that I didn't have talent and there wouldn't be a future in it. I went to school for graphic design and did terribly at it before working for a couple years at a beer company. I had a friend and mentor, Kellie, at the time who listened to me when I said I did love drawing but wouldn't do it because of my lack of skill, and she gave me some comics and encouraged me to go for it. At that time, I went all-in on becoming a comics inker. I had a webcomic when everybody had a webcomic some years ago, and I wanted to work with ink and digital color and stumbled on a small school in Florida doing a workshop for comics.

They had a library of comics, and I got to really immerse myself in different styles and techniques. One of the teachers did a focus on looking at old paintings, which, at first, I lost interest in, but the one lecture on 19th-century paintings changed everything for me. I studied French comics and loved how Lewis Trondheim used watercolor to color his comics. I decided to try it, and I never looked back. I became instantly obsessed—pardon the pun—like a fish in water, consuming all I could of 19th-century paintings and watercolor artists. The biggest change for me was the discovery of Cyril Pedrosa's Portugal. I basically quit comics after reading it. I stopped the webcomic I was working on and started doing drills and academic drawing and painting exercises all day, every day, eventually finding my way back to little journal comics, trying to take all these lessons I had been consuming in old paintings and figure out how to use them in comics. All of my professional comics work through the past few years stemmed from the mountain of rejections I got from Kodi when I first pitched it, which was a lesson in itself. It felt like a journey and the book Kodi was the result of my exploration.

*Kodi has such a unique visual design. What inspired this?*
**Jared Cullum:** Two main principles guided my concept and execution of the art in Kodi. The first is that I tried to always consider the world through the lens of the protagonist. I want the reader to get a similar feeling to the main girl walking through this world. Do you remember when you're a kid and you hold your dad's hand, or finger rather, and everything just seems so big? I tried to distort and design the world around that idea. The bear is larger than life.

Secondly, the world is built on shape feelings, which is a time-honored principle you find exemplified in Disney and other great character designs. Not to get too much into the boring sausage-making information, but the circle is generally a softer and friendly shape, so the grandmother is built entirely out of concentric circles focused on third-placement and the structural golden spiral equation. It makes her feel odd yet friendly and loveable. Triangles are more generally used as danger or off-kilter whereas squares are generally more unchanging and slow (think old man from Up!). Because I wanted Katya to represent a girl that is off-kilter but kind and loveable at heart, her design is built on the juxtaposition of circle against triangle. She wears a jacket that is generally a large triangle, and for the first three-quarters of the book she is generally posed in a way that structures her lower portion in a triangle against her round head.

*Please tell us about your creative process.*
**Jared Cullum:** My creative process is built on a lot of life-drawing and painting outside of comics. I attend as many live life-drawing sessions as possible. I generally collect plein air paintings and, until the pandemic, was an avid teacher locally of plein air painting (outdoors, on location). I spend a great deal of my time studying 19th-century paintings and the tools they used for storytelling. People like Jean-Léon Gérôme and John Singer Sargent are some favorites. I love to do small copies of their work to develop intuition for shape and color mixing. My focus is on light. Lighting a scene is one of the strongest storytelling elements that interests me.

Writing is the most difficult part for me. I'm not very good with words, as you can probably tell from my previous answers, so I rely on storyboarding and writing key scenes. I have to see the story and then add words, as reading and writing has always been difficult for me.

*What draws you to the comics medium?*

**Jared Cullum:** I deeply love the completely open sandbox that is comics. I love that you could essentially do the same thing I spent years on, developing Kodi, with just stick figures because to me, it is all the same. Shape and symbols as tools for connecting with other humans.

Whether I'm painting a location in front of me or trying to draw comics, the principle is similar. I'm trying to take the immense complexity of the world and condense it into something clear and readable to tell a story. When painting a figure or a landscape, I have value as my tool for simplification. With cartoons, I have shape and symbol and that toolbox can be used to any degree of complexity to share a story.

Every cartoonist has a toolbox, to borrow an analogy from Stephen King's On Writing. You have shape, composition, light, emotion, words, and you use them to solve whatever story problem. With comics, I can take the story anywhere and to any time I can imagine.

*What is your message for young comics makers?*

**Jared Cullum:** Enjoy the process and focus on whatever makes you passionate. Try to find a source of good clean fuel for your tank. For me, I have a safe harbor in traditional painting. It's a place I can go with no editors and no expectations. I can grow and experiment on my own terms, and I don't have to share it with anyone. I have also discovered a deep passion for European art of the late 19th century, but it wouldn't have happened if I decided I was going to be an inker and only focused on that. Try out various art forms and discover your own mentors to influence your stylistic choices. Finally, from a technical standpoint, learn to love life-drawing. You may not have any interest in "realistic" drawing, but drawing from life helps on a number of different levels. You can increase your drafting skills and also your connection to the world around you. It also increases your ability to sit and draw, and if you want to make comics . . . you're going to have to learn to sit and draw . . . a lot. My suggestion—and how I started drawing on advice from a friend—is to get a secret sketchbook no one is allowed to see. Draw only in ink and don't erase anything. The purpose is to learn problem solving and to work with your lines instead of seeing anything as a "mistake." It also gets you past the fear of the blank page as well as the attachment to individual drawings. Lastly, as you move to more professional-level work, develop a circle of trust you can share ideas with and be open and willing to accept criticism from.

*What message would you send to teachers who are planning to use your book in class?*

**Jared Cullum:** Well, thank you, humbly and sincerely, for thinking the book is worth sharing. I think the thing I'd like to impart to teachers is that the book is essentially a metaphor for me and my own journey into rediscovery of art. I think that every kid and person is a hero with their own fascinating Campbellian journey that can express through whatever art form spins off of their life. Mine just happens to be watercolor.

# Exploring Pathways of Storytelling: Verse Novels, Adaptations, and More

- *Learning for Justice—Diversity Anchor Standard 7. Students will develop language and knowledge to accurately and respectfully describe how people (including themselves) are both similar to and different from each other and others in their identity groups.*

Just as Victoria Jamieson and Omar Mohamed collaborated with words and pictures to tell Mohamed's story, there is textual work for reading and composing as hybridized and democratizing collaborative spaces for the merging of modes, formats, and styles. It is a delight when books treat us with the unexpected, and we can then be surprised alongside our students by what an author does.

Vasquez et al. (2019) give educators much to think about related to the identities represented in classrooms and how vital critical literacy is; along with this focus, Lankshear and Knobel (2011) can help us think about how images and digital texts, including comics and video games, work. While I honor the written word, I also appreciate art and digital storytelling, and I recognize that I work with a wide range of students who have particular experiences and interests. Moreover, my students are living in a world where information is delivered in many ways. If I am going to be a critical educator, I have to teach students to read the word and, as Paulo Freire put it, the world. This idea of reading the world or thinking about real-life connections and power structures also means reading the digital world now, too.

Returning to some of the questions from the first section of the book, in this chapter I explore the ways hybridized texts can be drawn upon in comics with attention to invitations to composition across both visuals and poetic structuring. While poetry is often taught separately, if at all, I recognize that uniting modes and methods of composition with the comics medium can help students see poetry in new ways.

I am a comics fan as well as an appreciator of verse. Both poetry and images have a powerful way of helping access emotions and allow for layers of processing experiences. It has been heartening to see the joining together of poetic work found in verse novels with the illustrative power of comics/graphic novels in recent adaptations. Poetry, in itself, can be used in a variety of ways—from sharing personal experiences to supporting research (Faulkner, 2017). Dav Pilkey illustrates this approach for us in his choice to include haikus in the Cat Kid Comic Club series. Pilkey combines the comics visual, even in cartoonish form, with the haiku in a way that does not position this poetic form as something ancient and unobtainable; it is as fun and lively as the rest of the Comic Club creative world. There are increasing numbers of adapted verse novels in graphic novel format. As author Jason Reynolds points out, verse novels offer an inviting format for readers who might be intimidated by the presence of many words on the page.

There are considerable possibilities for poetic adaptation in graphic novel form. While comics are flexible in their own right as a medium as far as both audience and the ways creators can make meaning through them, this flexibility only increases when the creators use the medium to tell new kinds of stories, including narrative poetry. The mainstay of my youth was the comics adaptation of popular movies, but comics can support a variety of adaptations.

In this chapter, I highlight the work of Kwame Alexander and the subsequent adaptation of his verse novels in graphic novel form. I once more foreground composing practices, noting the power of writing/creating afforded by the words, pictures, and grammatical elements found in the graphic novel medium.

## Connecting to Texts and Textual Links

Building on the opportunities for thinking about what is possible in comics through texts like *Cat Kid Comic Club* and *When Stars Are Scattered*, there are additional possibilities made available in verse novel texts. It is always my aim that students also see these possibilities and begin to experiment with layers of storytelling they might have previously seen as incompatible. In an ideal classroom, all modes of inquiry and composition, across reading and writing activities and experiences, flow together.

As one example of Kwame Alexander's work, I point to *The Crossover* comics adaptation, illustrated by Dawud Anyabwible (2014). The book includes poetry displayed in a comics script typography alongside images that support the poetic/narrative message. Readers can see the juxtaposition of words and images in poetic form, exploring the way a stanza might be presented in a multimodal format. Arguably, the shape of poetry itself is a visual form that can convey meaning both in alignment as well as in contradiction to elements of the poet's message. As is the case with concrete poetry, the poem's shape itself often reflects the topic.

This presentation of form can help teachers expand definitions and understandings of poetry beyond traditional approaches to teaching, which often means that words from hundreds of years ago are used as examples of poetry. Teachers can recenter instruction on contemporary voices and experiences. These experiences can be shown in verse that vibrates with today's world.

As an educator who advocates for students writing every day, I note that poetry provides a packed form that can deliver emotional complexity in a short space, taking up little class time. The span of time it takes to develop a focused, four-part or multi-paragraph essay is limiting both when thinking about compositional frameworks and about what can be done according to the clock. Poetry, on the other hand, can be less constrained than routinized approaches to writing, and it can even be a space to explore emotions and aspects of life that otherwise might not feel as welcome to unpack in a classroom setting.

Readers who do immediately engage with poetic form may approach verse with more fondness as a result of these kinds of visual renderings. Some readers who are not familiar with comics pages may also find the busyness of the pages distracting. It should also be noted that some verse novel adaptations abridge the original work from poets. Some readers may prefer the complete original versions, and the goal is always simply to read (though I would love for everyone to enjoy comics as much as I do).

This work is centered on the notion that teachers and students have connections with other members of the human family and that members of our classroom communities bring rich and diverse resources for our common learning experiences. Educators exist with students in co-construction and in conversation. Moreover, the literacy practices our students bring are rich and diverse, interconnected, and sites of celebration.

## Classroom Application Ideas

Educators use media to engage students in the powerful cognitive work that is part of adapting one mode of communication to another. As one example from my classroom, students read the novel *A Wrinkle in Time* by Madeleine L'Engle (1962) and adapted this classic, canonical young adult text to comics form for key scenes. Our classroom work took place years before Hope Larson published an adaptation of the book in graphic novel form.

Such publication does not limit the opportunity to adapt a work but rather adds another layer of possibility for ELA teachers. When reading a text that has been adapted multiple times, students can experience the text in its original form in addition to whatever media permutations are available. This work enables students to construct their own vision of what an adaptation might be like— and then check out how their rendition stacks up with a published form. In this way, the reading experience can be enriched. When trying this approach with students, teachers could lead their class in finding inquiry topics. Students can then follow up by exploring poetic examples, media, and images to collect examples of how a work has been adapted—culminating in their own unique adaptation. Texts, in this way, do not occupy an isolated position but reach across to complement, challenge, and affirm one another, as in the work of Ciecierski (2017).

As a strategy, I embrace the idea of "word harvest," in which students listen to the poetry that is being read to them—lots of love for the idea of having authors' voices spoken in classrooms through online videos and audio recordings!—and collect words that stand out to them. The following poem was captured in one of my classes after a listening session with the poem "Human Family" by Maya Angelou (1999) (underlined words were part of Angelou's original work):

### An Ode to Self-Care

An <u>Obvious</u> need to take time away,
<u>Beige</u>, the walls of my heart, burdens

A sinking daily <u>Profundity</u> removed, but not meaningless –
Do we have this in <u>Common</u>?
Ten thousand wounds, wound up, bound up, binding,
Our <u>Features</u> hidden by questions and careless comments?

Or am I alone, a soul walking by themselves, In <u>Serious</u> silent
   contemplation?
I <u>Thrive</u> on the knowledge I am not alone

Major or minor, we are the stars in our story,
<u>Alike</u>, as Maya said, <u>more than unalike</u>, joined in our common
   frailty and stronger in our lifting each other up.

I can next envision the poem as a visual form, crafted with images that provide another link both for the poet/teacher to explore and express and for the reader to relate to and/or reflect on experiences they share or that exist in contrast. I created the example in Figure 14.1, which features a poem that was written while facilitating a virtual clinic session in 2020. The words of the poem reflect the time and contrast the image of the heroic figure, attempting to ensure pedagogical delivery in a challenging time.

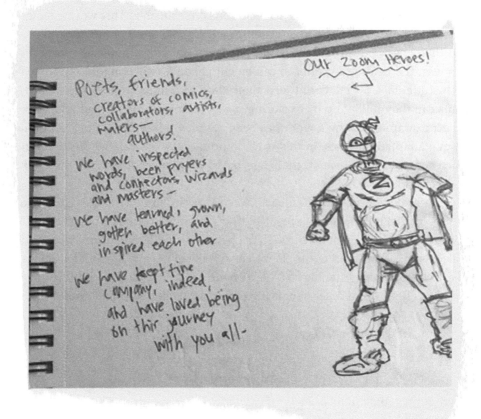

**FIGURE 14.1.** Author-Created Poem and Image Juxtaposition

# Steps for Further Work (Including Additional Resources/Book Titles)

I recommend exploring a range of verse novels, graphic novels, poetry collections, and texts that fuse these compositional approaches together. The collection *Poems to See By* (Peters, 2020), for example, is a treatment of classic verses from poets like Emily Dickinson along with images to capture the force of the poetry included. I also recommend teaching approaches like the inspirational take of the Visual Verse website (https://visualverse.org/), a site that (at the time of this writing) presents an image each month to inspire writers around the world.

There are a number of additional approaches that young creators can take in classroom spaces, including:

**Links to Visual Poetry with Students**: Ask students to compose poetic responses within the panels of comics or in other forms in response to images they find in texts. These can be visually based responses, linked to new words that students are learning, or images crafted by authors in the texts they are reading or curating.

**Illustrating Poetry:** In the opposite direction, young readers and composers can take existing poetry and adapt it to a visual form. I note that my definition of *poetry* includes works by classical poets, contemporary poets, writers for children, and even contemporary songwriters. Adapting popular music to visual form can form the basis for lessons based on figurative language and can help students redefine poetry in relevant ways. What's more, this approach can tap into youth fandom (Hagood et al., 2010).

**Drawing and Music:** Finally, poetic arrangements found in music can serve as part of the atmosphere of creation. Teachers can try out different "soundtracks of the moment" as students compose and later check in as part of whole-class narrative sharing or small-group/individual conferences to ask about how the music impacted the student's process. Music can be seen as influence in the student art featured in Figure 14.2.

**FIGURE 14.2.** Student-Created Example Featuring Billie Eilish

## Adaptations and Comics

Stories rarely appear in only one format these days, as publishers know full well the marketability results of engaging with fan culture. Comics can be read as standalone texts in classrooms, or they can be seen as paired texts. While reading a book and watching the film is a popular approach (Green et al., 2011), exploring multimodal and multimedia representations of the same story is another potential avenue for rich study across types of texts.

Verrone's (2013) consideration of adaptation theory can be helpful in thinking about how creators move stories across media, making decisions about what to abridge, add, or cut. While Verrone typically focuses on film adaptations, time works differently in comics. The ways media can create opportunities for adaptation depends a great deal on how the medium is designed and what tools for meaning-making are employed as part of its structure (Tseng & Bateman, 2018).

Teachers can guide students in a close reading of each kind of media and can position reading as a practice that encompasses a wide variety of engagements with texts, even from the beginning of the school year. Open thinking about texts can help us connect students with engaging work, even outside of school-based reading practices. All of our students are readers, even if this reading occurs in digital spaces or in ways that are not prioritized by traditional views of text.

Books are books, and reading is reading. For a lesson sequence navigating different approaches to the same story, there is no written rule. I am drawn to approaches that consider the books page by page and scene by scene, allowing some moments to be experienced first in prose, then in film, and then in visual format, or in different order depending on the emphasis that each scene holds. The creative decisions of artists and auteurs can be explored, including student responses and discussion about why changes are made from one medium to another.

I am also drawn to an approach in which students create their own comic adaptations without seeing the existing adaptation first followed by opportunities for comparing and contrasting. In the same way that readers sometimes "cast" a film version of a book while reading, educators can work with students in building visual models of what elements of a story might look like. Students may be surprised to find that they created work in the same way that a comics artist did—or that they discovered a different and equally valid or stylized way to capture the same moment or meaning.

I conclude this chapter with an interview segment with author/artist Alex-

**TABLE 14.1.** A List of Additional Adaptations.

| Adaptation | Features |
|---|---|
| *Turtle in Paradise* by Jennifer Holm, adapted by Savanna Ganucheau (2021) | Nominated for the 2021 Excellence in Graphic Literature Award, Middle Grades Category. The book works as a standalone for readers who are not familiar with the source material. |
| *The City of Ember* by Jeanne DuPrau, adapted by Dallas Maddaugh and Niklas Asker (2004) | DuPrau's Ember series was an imaginative entry in my middle grades classroom. The book, graphic novel adaptation, and film adaptation form a linked set of storytelling leading to later books in the series. |
| *The Metamorphosis* by Franz Kafka, adapted by Peter Kuper (2004) | The book itself is a strange wonder, part science fiction/fantasy, and part literary fiction. Kuper's unique style is on full display here and is worth noting in work for older readers, including his adaptation of Conrad's *Heart of Darkness* (2019). |
| *Coraline* by Neil Gaiman, adapted by P. Craig Russell (2009) | The haunting characters and world of Neil Gaiman are adapted here in a book that feels like it could have been written strictly for the graphic novel form (Gaiman's popular DC/Vertigo series *Sandman* precedes the popularity of his prose work). |
| *The Graveyard Book* by Neil Gaiman, adapted by P. Craig Russell (2017) | The book won a Harvey and an Eisner Award. Another entry into the world of Neil Gaiman, with the atmosphere and mood the author creates adapted in vivid style. |
| *The Giver* by Lois Lowry, adapted by P. Craig Russell (2020) | Russell takes the often-assigned novel by Lowry and lends his skill to a realistic and vivid alternative future. The artist captures moments in the narrative, like the passage of memories, in a clear visual way. |
| *The Great Gatsby* by F. Scott Fitzgerald, adapted by Fred Fordham and Aya Morton (2020) | The colorful spreads in the book are evocative of a range of moods, allowing for discussion of the time period and the emotional effect of the novel. |
| *Fahrenheit 451* by Ray Bradbury, adapted by Tim Hamilton (2009) | Hamilton takes the sometimes-poetic prose of Bradbury and illustrates it vividly, using reds and dark colors to evoke the mood that the book creates. |
| *Slaughterhouse-Five* by Kurt Vonnegut, adapted by Ryan North and Albert Monteys (2021) | North and Monteys do the almost unthinkable and take the strange, visceral, and beautiful work of Vonnegut, with all of its gallows humor and nonlinear narrative, and cast it in visual form. |

is E. Fajardo, whose Kid Beowulf series is an homage to the great epic stories of the world. Four of Fajardo's covers can be seen in Figure 14.3. It is intended to introduce young readers to ancient stories in a fun and accessible manner using comics.

**FIGURE 14.3.** Images Courtesy of Alexis Fajardo

## Words from Alexis E. Fajardo

**Alexis Fajardo:** *Kid Beowulf* comes from a combination of the things I grew up reading and loving: mythology and comics. Visually, it's inspired by the French series Asterix as well as American comic books and comic strips. Originally, when I began my comics career, I wanted to be a syndicated cartoonist and create a comic strip of my own for newspapers. Graphic novels were not as prevalent when I was younger, but I have a distinct memory of reading *The Dark Knight Returns* as a graphic novel, and it blew my mind. It was cinematic and unique because Frank Miller presented a story with a beginning, middle, and an end. He took comics to another level, and I distinctly remember the feeling of "whoa, comics can do anything!" Those disparate influences went into my creative melting pot. Eventually, I realized that comic strips were too constrictive for the kinds of stories I wanted to do, and graphic novels were where my storytelling strengths resided.

I read the epic poem *Beowulf* in my senior year of high school, and I may have been the only person in class who liked it. Prior to that I read adaptations of *The Odyssey* and *The Iliad,* but they were novelizations. *Beowulf* was the first time I read epic poetry, and it lit my brain on fire. The imagery was evocative and crystalline—I could see everything being described: the boats on the "the whale road," the confrontation between Beowulf and Grendel, the fire-snakes slithering in the mere [i.e., Grendel's cave]. The story had a visceral and primal quality that stood out to me. In college, I studied classics where I read *The Iliad* and *The Odyssey*, in some cases translating the ancient Greek to get the real flavor and power of those stories. I've always loved the old stories, so years later when I was rereading *Beowulf,* an odd notion struck me: what would the hulking Viking warrior Beowulf been like as a kid? It seemed immediately funny to me. I went further and made arch-enemies Beowulf and Grendel into twin brothers. The first iterations of the comic were comedic and satirical, but the more I kept working with the original text, more serious themes about culture, feuds, and magic began to surface in my writing.

I decided that the Kid Beowulf series would follow the adventures of twin brothers Beowulf and Grendel as they traveled the world and met fellow epic heroes therein. I would use the epic poem *Beowulf* as a gateway to the other epics of the world. I wanted to have conversations with these old stories through my comics and show readers how the epics are similar, where they diverge, and ultimately, inspire them to read and explore the original stories for themselves.

# Conclusion: A Graphic Novel Critical/Pedagogic Creed

As a conclusion to this book, I emphasize the next steps in the layered and considerate process of using graphic novels for literacy instruction across grade levels. It is also my aim to provide a summary of why graphic novels should have a place in instruction. Once more, this work has been written with the framework in mind of providing opportunities for students to, quite literally, see themselves represented in a text in a way that is unique to graphic novels and comics. I use the term "text" widely and with great passion as I work to discover (re)presentations of lived experiences in prose, poetry, images, and digital spaces.

In defense of a graphic novel pedagogy, Brozo (2013) has noted that these works have the potential to build engagement across content areas and to offer invitations to complex concepts in meaningful ways. Yet these books are not naturally implemented in pedagogy without some consideration and even training in their proper usage (Lapp et al., 2012). Encountering a graphic novel is a deceptively complex task for both student and teacher. Comics can tell a variety of stories and link to classroom conversations about relevant topics. What's more, comics are ripe for instruction addressing comprehension, fluency, vocabulary, and composing. Comics are not just about superheroes these days; they are, indeed, texts that can lead to critical conversations, flexible in both their design and when considering their potential audience. They can share personal stories or global ones, realistic stories or fantastic ones. Comics can teach.

There is no particular assumed audience for comics, as they are popular across age groups, even into adulthood. This is an idea borne out by the work of Stergios Botzakis and is reflected on shelves in bookstores and in classroom libraries around the world. Given the possibilities for representation of cultural, gender, political, and racial/ethnic intersections of identity presented in visual format over the past decade, that audience has become much more inclusive.

The popularity of these books with a wide range of readers was evident in my classroom and continues to be revealed by the ways that readers take up these books and engage with them. My first teaching steps in a graphic novel-centered pedagogy came at the end of my second year of teaching when, in the strange space of the time after the summative state test, I commissioned students with the task of creating their own comic strips to reflect literary elements. This experience of students making comics, sometimes unprompted in the classroom, is one that I found popular, creative, and appealing for many students, so I continued the work and expanded the ideas I tried out.

When I turned my attention to university instruction in 2015, multimodal texts had been gaining prominence for about four or five years, and graphic novels were increasingly available in school book fairs and in some classroom spaces. Raina Telgemeier was known in the middle school reading arena, but there was a very present tension between the then-prevalent notion of complex reading that was encouraged by my school district's interpretation of the Common Core initiative and texts that did not lend themselves easily to Lexile measures.

It was in this context that I was encouraged to stray from my readings with students of more popular texts and include more classics and literature that was deemed as "higher level." At one time, it might have been difficult to imagine that a multimodal, digital, or graphic novel-centered pedagogy could become a focus for instruction or that my use of these texts could be implemented beyond engagement in choice reading times and in the context of student-led projects. I often failed to highlight these texts prominently, given the pushback I received on prose novels that did not reach a particular Lexile level. In fact, my journey as a teacher educator has led me back to a K–12 classroom, where I continue to explore these ideas. The projects students co-constructed with digital tools have often relied on the presence of a "real book" like a prose novel to justify their presence. Sometimes they were the fun activities we engaged with after the high-stakes test was completed. However, comics can stand on their own as useful resources for building literacy instruction.

Part of the plight of the education professor is the desire to reach back and tell the former teaching self to try out new ideas and texts that are only discovered and appreciated later, and the joy is that I now get to engage with this work in classrooms with my own adolescent students. The story also continues, and I have now shared these strategies and approaches more widely with preservice and inservice teachers in several postsecondary classes.

## The Reading Continues and the Conversation Continues

The stories I have highlighted in this book merely scratch the surface of the growing number of available texts, and I hope that this area of literature expands more and more. As I prepare this conclusion, I recognize that there are a number of new graphic novels on the horizon. To be honest, it is difficult to keep up, and I am constantly perusing Amazon lists, Goodreads, Book Riot, and NetGalley as sources for thinking about what is soon to be published or what I may have missed. I still run across a book that has been out for a while that somehow eluded my searching.

This book has been a reflection on considerable time spent reading and discussing comics and graphic novels alongside students and colleagues, and it comes from a commitment to the joy of discovery in books. Sometimes that joy also contains painful truth as teachers encounter voices that have long been silenced or when students and teachers consider the ways that policies attempt to eclipse the experiences of some voices.

Sometimes critical issues and conversations, along with the intersections of identity that students carry with them and that are represented in their families, are erased by educational policies and practices. We must advocate for doing better.

Much of this book centers around the work I have continued to do with comic books, graphic novels, and other visual texts. A significant part of this work has taken place in digital spaces within the context of the move to virtual instruction, but our collective work began months prior to this time. Based on this in-person and virtual work, this seems to be a pressing and prescient time to talk about comics. In this book, I have explored this medium with flexibility across the ages/genders/identities of potential readers, the visual and verbal possibilities for representations of lived experience as well as content for comprehension, and the implications of using graphic novels in literacy instruction.

How has this medium informed teaching practices?

## Tenets of Comics in the Classroom

- Comics allow readers to explore and express ideas in visual format. In Figure 15.1, a student creator illustrates their understanding of the novel, *Fahrenheit 451*, through digital art.

- Comics act as visual means of exploring characters and settings. In Figure 15.2, a student crafts an imagined travel log.

- Comics allow for avenues of culture/world-building and world-based exploration.

- Comics contain unique designs for literacy instruction, including popular characters and more.

- Comics, like all texts, have limitations.

- Comics can be used to tell narratives as well as convey information.

**FIGURE 15.1.** Student-Created Collage Response to *Fahrenheit 451*

**FIGURE 15.2.** Student-Created Travelogue Comic

From this last point, we can consider the voice of comics writer Jason Viola, contributor to the Science Comics series. Viola explores and practices the incorporation of informational text in comics form.

## Words from Jason Viola about Comics and Informational Text

*How did you find your way to comics?*

**Jason Viola:** When I was a kid, as young as I can remember, I loved reading and drawing comics. I made up a comic strip called "Acronym" which was basically just Garfield except he was a bird instead of a cat. Instead of hating Mondays, Acronym hated Wednesdays. Pretending it was published in wide circulation, I drew a new one every day, collected them in books, drew wall calendars and holiday specials. I knew for sure I wanted to be a cartoonist when I grew up.

When I got older, I tried getting into superhero comics for a couple years, and then in high school I just grew out of it. I wasn't exposed to many comics for adults, and '90s bookstores hardly had "graphic novels" sections. I grew disillusioned with my art classes and decided that writing would be my focus, not art. I had a lot of fun with writing that I no longer found in drawing.

Years later, I realized that it was because I'd completely dropped the storytelling aspect of drawing. All the drawings I made as a kid were in the service of characters and stories. But in high school, it was just figures in space—a portrait, a still life, a three-point perspective exercise. Rediscovering comics as an adult made me realize what I'd been missing. A friend turned me onto an Alan Moore book and it made me curious about what else my library had. And I completely fell in love again, devouring everything on those four shelves. I didn't know what was out there or what my taste was, and just read everything I could find. After a year or so of reading, I really wanted to make comics again. And I soon found a home in comics communities, online and at festivals.

*What is your creative process like?*

**Jason Viola:** A new idea comes with questions to answer, or problems to solve. When you have a problem, it's helpful to talk about it, and for me it's especially helpful to write about it. Writing about my problem in a letter or email to someone often leads me to an answer or perspective I hadn't seen before. I've turned this strategy into my standard writing process. I write a kind of letter to myself in a very conversational way. "So. I need to get from point A to point B. But if I just do this one thing, then it won't make sense because of this other thing. What if I do X and Y? Hmm. That might work but only if I can establish Z first. Hey, maybe if I put Z first then I can do this other thing. Part of me wonders if . . . " and so on. Being so informal about it frees me up to just keep writing, keep moving, and I always get somewhere eventually. And then I can write the story bits, sometimes continuing to add these notes to myself in between just to break the silence.

The goal is to get in that "flow" state which is hard to do by staring at a blank screen. I know no one will ever see this weird diary of mine and this technique guides me to a place where I can think more creatively.

*What do comics allow you to do in informational writing?*
**Jason Viola:** Comics excel at communicating complex ideas and breaking down processes, making them more tangible. At MICE (the Massachusetts Independent Comics Expo), I helped produce a podcast episode that explores how that works. There's a lot that could be said about this, so I'm just going to pick one aspect.

Personally, I love that First Second's Science Comics series leverages stories and characters to educate. At an elementary school talk I did, one of the students asked, "Are these books fiction or nonfiction?" The book I was presenting is full of true facts about polar bears but disguised in stuff I made up. Our polar bears are characters with their own names, desires, and anxieties, who grow and change. And they talk, which is not scientifically accurate. It's similar to the way kids learn about their world by playing pretend. It's fun but also functional.

Global warming is a big concept that a lot of us have trouble grasping. But by learning about transparent polar bear fur and the absorptive properties of their black skin, it becomes easier to understand how albedo accelerates climate change in the Arctic. In the book, we discover the different kinds of sea ice that make up the bears' world (I had no idea there were so many kinds of ice). And we realize that the ice isn't just the place they go to hunt; the microorganisms that live on the underside of the ice are the foundation of the entire Arctic food web. We follow the cubs as they learn how to thrive in their environment, and by the end we're rooting for their survival. The loss of sea ice becomes a very real threat.

I'm grateful that it can work so well, because stories and characters are really where my heart is.


# Why Now?

First, I hope it is clear and always possible that we can push back against any voices that would seek to diminish the identities of people of minoritized communities. Similarly, educators can (and should) push back against anyone who seeks to downplay the power of reading choice and multimodal methods of storytelling as critical ways to engage a flexible audience in flexible literacies.

In addition to the impact these books have made upon my life and the lives of students (and comics creators) I have met, there are a number of reasons why visual reading is important at the moment and why I contend that graphic novels, the term often used for longer books in the comics medium, will be useful for some time to come. As mentioned earlier, I have seen readers cross rooms to check out the newest graphic novel I bring with me when I have visited classrooms. I have observed the empty space on the classroom and clinic shelves as readers frequently return to the same texts, and graphic novels circulate among students and colleagues. I have happened upon the spontaneous comics creations of students, tucked away in notebooks without my involvement.

Jovanovic and Van Leeuwen's (2018) consideration of multimodal discourse in socially constructed digital spaces serves as another part of the foundation in my thinking. The emotive possibilities contained in multimodal literature, as meaning is born out through words, images, and other features, can serve as a powerful connection even when teaching online. Whether presented in a digital form or printed copy, graphic novels are welcoming spaces of literacy interaction for students of all ages.

The theory of multimodality, explored and implemented by literacy scholars like Gunther Kress and Jennifer Rowsell, can be helpful in thinking about how meaning is communicated on the comics/graphic novels page. Kress is one of the primary voices in this theory, noting how authors share meanings through words, images, gestures, design, and more. While a traditional prose or poetic text offers words only and an illustrated novel offers separate entities of word and picture, the graphic novel page offers a marriage of the two. In a 2020 article, Rowsell noted how adolescent writers use composing across modes (or ways of meaning-making), including the emotions and viewpoints that the young authors were able to explore through multimodal texts. You will note that many of the examples I have included reflect a range of identities and include thoughtful work in race, ethnicity, gender, culture, and other aspects of identity. It should also be noted that these are increasingly important, albeit sometimes uncomfortable, conversations for teachers to have. Part of the work that is essential with text is also context found in developing conversations and well-crafted questions and literacy strategies.

Graphic novels are powerful not only in the way they are made up but in the work they do philosophically and ideologically. As Bishop (1990) has suggested, seeing ourselves represented in text, as well as glimpsing the lives that challenge our assumptions and norms, is paramount.

## Moving Forward in Context

Tovani (2000) has noted the reality of "fake reading," and this idea can lead to a range of experiences, from renewed engagement with some tools for new purposes to the phenomenon of some students disappearing from the teacher's view completely. In thinking and practice, multimodal texts are now more central than ever, and the changing nature of instruction within digital contexts that Leu et al. (2018) have described is all the more palpable.

### Possibilities in Pedagogy with Multimodal Texts

1. That multimodal instruction can be meaningfully highlighted in the curriculum.
2. That comic books and graphic novels are rich texts that can lead to engaging and enriching experiences for readers of all ages.
3. That an increased awareness of students as authors and navigators of the digital and multimodal textual world be present in classroom practice.
4. That we continue to explore possibilities for increased access to a wide range of books for learners of all ages.

**FIGURE 15.3.** A List of Comics Commitments.

As has been the case with many of the chapters in this book, I conclude with an author interview, this time focused on the writing and plotting part of the comics-making process from a voice who has moved from prose to comics. I have learned from discussions with comics artists and authors that making these books is a multistep process that differs among the individual creator and that a host of materials are used. Composing (and reading) comics is far from simple work.

Sometimes, authors prefer digital ways of creating. Others are "old school" and draw everything out by hand, forcing themselves to re-create entire pages if one part of the work needs fixing.

In all cases, it is my desire to honor the reading, composing, and com-municating practices of all students, and I continue to read, learn, and grow. The final word in this text now arrives from comics writer Michael Northrop, in which he discusses both his reading/literacy history as well as his writing progression. Northrop is the author of several prose novels, including the TombQuest series and the DC Comics books *Dear Justice League* and *Young Alfred: Pain in the Butler.*

## Words from Michael Northrop about Comics and Authoring

*Please tell us a bit about your author/creator origin story.*
**Michael Northrop:** It was definitely a circuitous route! I am dyslexic, spent time in special ed, and repeated second grade. The first things I read on my own were comic books and *Dungeons & Dragons* rulebooks. (I was basically tricked into it.) From there I gravitated toward poetry, because it's short and you have to read it slowly and carefully, which was the only way I could read anyway. I followed poetry into full-blown English department nerd-dom. I could never read as fast as my classmates, but spending so much time on each page helped me notice and remember more of what I read. My writing followed the same sort of progression: poems to short stories to longer stories to novellas to novels.

*What draws you to comics?*
**Michael Northrop:** My recent work in comics and graphic novels really feels like coming full circle to where I started. Comics were the first things I could read (almost) as fast as my friends and the first time I was on the same page (literally) as my classmates. It's a perfect medium for reluctant readers or readers struggling for whatever reason, whether that's a learning disability or a second language. So much of it is visual storytelling and intuitive in a way that feels more and more relevant to the tech-heavy, multimedia world we're living in.

*What is your message for young authors and creators?*
**Michael Northrop:** Apart from the usual (read! write! have fun!), I'd encourage young creators to finish projects. The beginning is the easy part—that fun new idea, that shiny new thing—but even when things bog down and get messy and you just want to give up and start something new, keep going. Because once you finish, you can start to revise. You can decide what works and what doesn't and figure out how to make it better. The end of the first draft is the start of what your project will become, and the revision is often as important as the writing.

# References

Abraham, S., & Kedley, K. (2021). You can't say pupusa without saying pupusa: Translanguaging in a community-based writing center. *Community Literacy Journal, 15*(1), 47–69.

Alexander, D. (2021). *Other boys.* First Second.

Baetens, J. (2011). From black & white to color and back: What does it mean (not) to use color? *College Literature, 38*(3), 111–128.

Bagieu, P. (2018). *Brazen: Rebel ladies who rocked the world.* First Second.

Becker, H. (2021). *Himawari house.* First Second.

Bell, C. (2014). *El deafo.* Harry N. Abrams.

Bezemer, J., & Kress, G. (2015). *Multimodality, learning and communication: A social semiotic frame.* Routledge.

Billen, M. T., Ward, N. A., DeHart, J. D., Moran, R. R., & Yang, S. (2022). Flipping the script of "official knowledge" through multimodal composition. *Kappa Delta Pi Record, 58*(2), 92–94.

Bishop, R. (1990, March). Windows and mirrors: Children's books and parallel cultures. In M. Atwell & A. Klein (Eds.), *California State University Reading Conference: 14th Annual Conference Proceedings,* 3–12. CSUSB Reading Conference.

Bishop, R. S. (2016). A ride with Nana and CJ: Engagement, appreciation, and social action. *Language Arts, 94*(2), 120–123.

Bjartveit, C. J., & Panayotidis, E. L. (2014). Pointing to Shaun Tan's *The Arrival* and re-imagining visual poetics in research. *Contemporary Issues in Early Childhood, 15*(3), 245–261.

Blabey, A. (2015). *The bad guys.* Scholastic.

Boerman-Cornell, W., & Kim, J. (2020). *Using graphic novels in the English language arts classroom.* Bloomsbury Academic.

Botzakis, S. (2009). Adult fans of comic books: What they get out of reading. *Journal of Adolescent & Adult Literacy, 53*(1), 50–59.

Botzakis, S. (2013). Why I teach comics in higher education: Finding truth, justice and literacy with graphic novels. *Knowledge Quest, 41*(3), 68–71.

Brosgol, V. (2018). *Be prepared*. First Second.

Brozo, W. G. (2013). From manga 2 math. *Educational Leadership, 71*(3), 58–61.

Buchholz, B. A., DeHart, J. D., & Moorman, G. (2020). Digital citizenship during a global pandemic: Moving beyond digital literacy. *Journal of Adolescent & Adult Literacy, 64*(1), 11–17.

Bui, T. (2018). *The best we could do: An illustrated memoir*. Abrams ComicArts.

Carleton, S. (2014). Drawn to change: Comics and critical consciousness. *Labour: Journal of Canadian Labour Studies/Le Travail: Revue d'Études Ouvrières Canadiennes, 73*, 151–177.

Case, J. (2022). *Little monarchs*. Margaret Ferguson Books.

Chase, M., Son, E. H., & Steiner, S. (2014). Sequencing and graphic novels with primary-grade students. *The Reading Teacher, 67*(6), 435–443.

Chau, A. (2021). *Marshmallow & Jordan*. First Second.

Chireau, Y. (2020). White or Indian? Whiteness and becoming the white Indian comics superhero. In S. Guynes & M. Lund (Eds.), *Unstable masks: Whiteness and American superhero comics* (pp. 193–211). Ohio State University Press.

Christmas, J. (2022). *Swim team*. Harper Alley.

Chute, H. (2008). Comics as literature? Reading graphic narrative. *Publications of the Modern Language Association of America, 123*(2), 452–465.

Ciecierski, L. M. (2017). What the Common Core State Standards do not tell you about connecting texts. *The Reading Teacher, 71*(3), 285–294.

Cocca, C. (2014). The 'Broke Back Test': A quantitative and qualitative analysis of portrayals of women in mainstream superhero comics, 1993–2013. *Journal of Graphic Novels and Comics, 5*(4), 411–428.

Cohn, N. (2018). In defense of a "grammar" in the visual language of comics. *Journal of Pragmatics, 127*, 1–19.

Comber, B., Janks, H., & Hruby, G. G. (2018). Texts, identities, and ethics: Critical literacy in a post-truth world. *Journal of Adolescent & Adult Literacy, 62*(1), 95–99.

Connors, S. P. (2015). Expanding students' analytical frameworks through the study of graphic novels. *Journal of Children's Literature, 41*(2), 5–15.

Craft, J. (2019). *New kid*. Quill Tree Books.

Craft, J. (2020, January 10). Comic relief. *The New York Times*. https://www.nytimes.com/2020/01/10/books/review/comic-relief.html

Cruse, H. (2020). *Stuck rubber baby* (25th anniversary ed.). First Second.

Cullum, J. (2020). *Kodi*. Top Shelf Productions.

Dallacqua, A. K. (2022). "Let me just close my eyes": Challenged and banned books, claimed identities, and comics. *Journal of Adolescent & Adult Literacy, 66*(2), 134–138. https://ila.onlinelibrary.wiley.com/doi/abs/10.1002/jaal.1250

Dallacqua, A. K., Kersten, S., & Rhoades, M. (2015). Using Shaun Tan's work to foster multiliteracies in 21st-century classrooms. *The Reading Teacher, 69*(2), 207–217.

Dallacqua, A. K., & Peralta, L. R. (2019). Reading and (re)writing science comics: A study of informational texts. *The Reading Teacher, 73*(1), 111–118.

Dauvillier, L. (2014). *Hidden: A child's story of the Holocaust* (M. Lizano & G. Salsedo, Illus.). First Second.

Deer, B. (2019). *The fox wife* (D. Herron, Illus.). Inhabit Media.

Dembicki, M. (Ed.) (2010). *Trickster: Native American tales, a graphic collection.* Chicago Review Press.

Duncan, R., Taylor, M. R., & Stoddard, D. (2015). *Creating comics as journalism, memoir and nonfiction.* Routledge.

Dunn, D., & Love, B. L. (2020). Antiracist language arts pedagogy is incomplete without Black joy. *Research in the Teaching of English, 55*(2), 190–192.

Dunn, M. B. (2021). When teachers hurt: Supporting preservice teacher well-being. *English Education, 53*(2), 145–151.

Dunn, M. B., & Garcia, A. (2020). Grief, loss, and literature: Reading texts as social artifacts. *The English Journal, 109*(6), 52–58.

Durand, E. (2021). *Parenthesis.* Top Shelf Productions.

Dutro, E. (2011). Writing wounded: Trauma, testimony, and critical witness in literacy classrooms. *English Education, 43*(2), 193–211.

Fajardo, A. (2016). *Kid Beowulf: The blood-bound oath.* Andrews McMeel Publishing.

Fajardo, A. (2021). *Hama the pig's big adventure.* Kid Beowulf Comics.

Farrell, M., Arizpe, E., & McAdam, J. (2010). Journeys across visual borders: Annotated spreads of "The Arrival" by Shaun Tan as a method for understanding pupils' creation of meaning through visual images. *The Australian Journal of Language and Literacy, 33*(3), 198–210.

Faulkner, S. L. (2016). *Poetry as method: Reporting research through verse.* Routledge.

Fernández, K. (2021). *Manu: A graphic novel.* Graphix.

Fredrickson, E. (2022, May 2). *Montana poets embrace Native culture in new graphic novel.* Montana Free Press. https://montanafreepress.org/2022/05/02/montana-poets-represent-native-culture-in-new-graphic-novel/

Gallagher, K. (2014). Making the most of mentor texts. *Educational Leadership, 71*(7), 28–33.

Gao, L. (2022). *Messy roots: A graphic memoir of a Wuhanese American.* Balzer + Bray.

García, O., Flores, N., Seltzer, K., Wei, L., Otheguy, R., & Rosa, J. (2021) Rejecting abyssal thinking in the language and education of racialized bilinguals: A manifesto. *Critical Inquiry in Language Studies, 18*(3), 203–228.

García, O., Lin, A. M., & May, S. (Eds.) (2017). *Bilingual and multilingual education* (3rd ed.). Springer.

Gavigan, K. (2012). Caring through comics: Graphic novels and bibliotherapy for grades 6–12. *Knowledge Quest, 40*(5), 78–80.

Geraghty, L. (2018). Nostalgia, fandom and the remediation of children's culture. In P. Booth (Ed.), *A companion to media fandom and fan studies* (pp. 161–174). Wiley-Blackwell.

Gillman, M. (2017). *As the crow flies*. Iron Circus Comics.

Glascock, J., & Preston-Schreck, C. (2004). Gender and racial stereotypes in daily newspaper comics: A time-honored tradition? *Sex Roles, 51*(7), 423–431.

Golding, S., & Verrier, D. (2021). Teaching people to read comics: The impact of a visual literacy intervention on comprehension of educational comics. *Journal of Graphic Novels and Comics, 12*(5), 824–836.

González, N., Moll, L. C., & Amanti, C. (Eds.). (2005). *Funds of knowledge: Theorizing practices in households, communities, and classrooms*. Routledge.

Gorman, A. (2021). *The hill we climb: An inaugural poem for the country*. Viking Books.

Green, J. P. (2020). *InvestiGators*. First Second.

Green, M. C., Kass, S., Carrey, J., Herzig, B., Feeney, R., & Sabini, J. (2008). Transportation across media: Repeated exposure to print and film. *Media Psychology, 11*(4), 512–539.

Hagood, M. C., Alvermann, D. E., & Heron-Hruby, A. (2010). *Bring it to class: Unpacking pop culture in literacy learning*. Teachers College Press.

Halse Anderson, L. (2018). *Speak: The graphic novel* (E. Carroll, Illus.). Farrar, Straus and Giroux.

Harper, C. (2021). *Bad sister* (R. Lucey, Illus.). First Second.

Hart, T. (2018). *The art of the graphic memoir: Tell your story, change your life*. St. Martin's Griffin.

Harvey, S., & Ward, A. (2017). *From striving to thriving: How to grow confident, capable readers*. Scholastic Professional.

Hatke, B. (2011). *Zita the spacegirl*. First Second.

Hatke, B. (2016). *Mighty Jack*. First Second.

Henzi, S. (2016). "A necessary antidote": Graphic novels, comics, and Indigenous writing. *Canadian Review of Comparative Literature/Revue Canadienne de Littérature Comparée, 43*(1), 23–38.

Hobbs, R. (2020). *Mind over media: Propaganda education for a digital age*. W. W. Norton & Company.

Holmes, M. (2021). *My own world*. First Second.

Holt, K.A. (2015). *Rhyme schemer*. Chronicle Books.

Horn, M., & Giacobbe, M. E. (2007). *Talking, drawing, writing: Lessons for our youngest writers*. Stenhouse Publishers.

Hughes, K. (2020). *Displacement*. First Second.

Husbye, N. E., Buchholz, B. A., Powell, C. W., & Vander Zanden, S. (2019). "Death didn't come up at center time": Sharing books about grief in elementary literacy classrooms. *Language Arts, 96*(6), 347–357.

Jenkins, H. (2020). *Comics and stuff*. New York University Press.

Jewell, T. (2020). *This book is antiracist: 20 lessons on how to wake up, take action, and do the work* (A. Durand, Illus.). Frances Lincoln Children's Books.

Johnson, V. (2020). *Twins* (S. Wright, Illus.). Graphix.

Johnson, V. (2022). *Mister Miracle: The great escape* (D. Isles, Illus.). DC Comics.

Jovanovic, D., & Van Leeuwen, T. (2018). Multimodal dialogue on social media. *Social Semiotics, 28*(5), 683–699.

Joy, A. (2020). *Black is a rainbow color* (E. Holmes, Illus.). Roaring Brook Press.

Judd, S. P., Jacob, T., & Perker, M. K. (2021). *The rez detectives: Justice served cold*. Literati Press Comics and Novels.

Judd, S. P., & Jacob, T. (2021). *The Rez detectives: Justice served cold* (M. Perker, Illus.). Literati Press Comics and Novels.

Kazoo Magazine. (2020). *Noisemakers: 25 women who raised their voices & changed the world—A graphic collection from Kazoo* (E. Bried, Ed.). Knopf Books for Young Readers.

Kendi, I. X. (2020). *Antiracist baby* (A. Lukashevsky, Illus.). Kokila.

Khor, S. Y. (2021). *The legend of Auntie Po*. Kokila.

Kim, J. (2017). *Where's Halmoni?* Little Bigfoot.

King, T. (2022). *Borders* (N. Donovan, Illus.). Little, Brown Ink.

Knisley, L. (2020). *Stepping stones*. Random House Graphic.

Kuh, L. P., Leekeenan, D., Given, H., & Beneke, M. R. (2016). Moving beyond antibias activities: Supporting the development of antibias practices. *Young Children, 71*(1), 58–65.

Lai, R. (2021). *Pawcasso*. Henry Holt and Co. BYR Paperbacks.

Lapp, D., Moss, B., & Rowsell, J. (2012). Envisioning new literacies through a lens of teaching and learning. *The Reading Teacher, 65*(6), 367–377.

Late Show with Stephen Colbert, The. (2021, December 3). *"There's nothing wrong with us"—Jason Reynolds says normalizing anxiety is a way to beat it* [Video]. YouTube. https://www.youtube.com/watch?v=nNzYE_4DdtA

Laurent Clerc National Deaf Education Center. (2022). *15 principles for reading to Deaf children.* https://clerccenter.gallaudet.edu/ndec/early-intervention/15-principles-for-reading-to-deaf-children/

Lê, M. (2018). *Drawn together* (D. Santat, Illus.). Little, Brown Books for Young Readers.

Lemieux, A., Smith, A., McLean, C., & Rowsell, J. (2020). Visualizing mapping as pedagogy for literacy futures. *Journal of Curriculum Theorizing, 35*(2), 1–23.

Letizia, A. (2020). Truth, politics and disability: Graphic narratives as illustrated hope. *The Comics Grid: Journal of Comics Scholarship, 10*(1). https://www.comicsgrid.com/articles/10.16995/cg.184

Leu, D. J., Kinzer, C. K., Coiro, J., Castek, J., & Henry, L. A. (2018). New literacies: A dual-level theory of the changing nature of literacy, instruction, and assessment. In D. Alvermann, N. Unrau, M. Sailors, & R. Ruddell (Eds.), *Theoretical Models and Processes of Literacy* (7th ed., pp. 319–346). Routledge.

Lewis, J., & Aydin, A. (2016). *March: Book one* (N. Powell, Illus.). Top Shelf Productions.

Lewis, J., & Aydin, A. (2021). *Run: Book one* (L. Fury & N. Powell, Illus.). Harry N. Abrahams.

Lewison, M., Leland, C., & Harste, J. C. (2014). *Creating critical classrooms: Reading and writing with an edge*. Routledge.

Love, B. (2020). *We want to do more than survive: Abolitionist teaching and the pursuit of educational freedom*. Beacon Press.

Mbalia, K. (2022). *Tristan Strong punches a hole in the sky: The graphic novel* (O. Stephens, Illus.). Disney-Hyperion Books.

McCloud, S. (1994). *Understanding comics: The invisible art*. William Morrow Paperbacks.

McFarlane, J. M. (2019). Using visual narratives (comics) to increase literacy and highlight stories of social justice: Awakening to truth and reconciliation. *Collected Essays on Learning and Teaching, 12*, 46–59.

McKinney, L. L. (2021). *Nubia: Real one* (R. Smith, Illus.). DC Comics.

Miller, K. (2020). *Act*. Clarion Books.

Miller, N. K. (2014). The trauma of diagnosis: Picturing cancer in graphic memoir. *Configurations, 22*(2), 207–223.

Moeller, R. (2011). "Aren't these boy books?": High school students' readings of gender in graphic novels. *Journal of Adolescent & Adult Literacy, 54*(7), 476–484.

Moeller, R., & Irwin, M. (2012). Seeing the same: A follow-up study on the portrayals of disability in graphic novels read by young adults. *School Library Research, 15*, 1–15.

Muhammed, G. (2020). *Cultivating genius: An equity framework for culturally and historically responsive literacy*. Scholastic Teaching Resources.

Murray, D. (2021). *Better place* (S. Daley, Illus.). Top Shelf Productions.

The New London Group. (1996). A pedagogy of multiliteracies: Designing social futures. *Harvard Educational Review, 66*(1), 60–93.

Nguyen, M. K. (2019). *Pilu of the woods*. Oni Press.

Nicholson, W. (1989). *Shadowlands*. Fireside Theatre.

Ohlhausen, M., & Jepsen, M. (1992). Lessons from Goldilocks: "Somebody's been choosing my books but I can make my own choices now!" *The New Advocate, 5*(1), 31–46.

Opitz, M. F., & Rasinski, T. V. (2008). *Good-bye round robin: 25 effective oral reading strategies*. Heinemann.

Ortega, C. (2022). *Frizzy* (R. Bousamra, Illus.). First Second.

Page, T. (2022). *Button pusher*. First Second.

Pahl, K. H., & Rowsell, J. (2011). Artifactual critical literacy: A new perspective for literacy education. *Berkeley Review of Education, 2*(2), 129–151.

Pahl, K., & Rowsell, J. (2019). *Artifactual literacies: Every object tells a story.* Teachers College Press.

Palacio, R. J. (2019). *White bird: A wonder story.* Knopf Books for Young Readers.

Pardeck, J. T. (1990). Using bibliotherapy in clinical practice with children. *Psychological Reports, 67*(3), 1043–1049.

Parker, K. N. (2022). *Literacy is liberation: Working toward justice through culturally relevant teaching.* ASCD.

Pennell, A. E., Wollak, B., & Koppenhaver, D. A. (2018). Respectful representations of disability in picture books. *The Reading Teacher, 71*(4), 411–419.

Peters, J. (2020). *Poems to see by: A comic artist interprets great poetry.* Plough Publishing House.

Philbrick, R. (2001). *Freak the mighty.* Scholastic.

Picower, B. (2021). *Reading, writing, and racism: Disrupting Whiteness in teacher education and in the classroom.* Beacon Press.

Pilkey, D. (2020). *Cat kid comic club.* Graphix.

Postema, B. (2014). Following the pictures: Wordless comics for children. *Journal of Graphic Novels and Comics, 5*(3), 311–322.

Powell, N. (2021). *Save it for later: Promises, parenthood, and the urgency of protest.* Harry N. Abrams.

Prater, M. A., Johnstun, M. L., Dyches, T. T., & Johnstun, M. R. (2006). Using children's books as bibliotherapy for at-risk students: A guide for teachers. *Preventing School Failure: Alternative Education for Children and Youth, 50*(4), 5–10.

Randall, R., & Mercurio, M. L. (2015). Valuing stuff: Materials culture and artifactual literacies in the classroom. *Journal of Adolescent & Adult Literacy, 59*(3), 319–327.

Rather, D., & Kirschner, E. (2021). *What unites us: The graphic novel* (T. Foley, Illus.). First Second.

Raúl the Third. (2021). *El Toro & friends: Tag team.* Versify.

Reece, C. (2015). *Metaphase.* Alterna.

Reid, S. F., & Moses, L. (2021). Rewriting deficit storylines: The positioning of one fourth-grader as comics expert. *English Teaching: Practice & Critique, 20*(3), 298–312.

Reynolds, J. (2021). *Stuntboy, in the meantime* (Raúl the Third, Illus.). Atheneum/Caitlyn Dlouhy Books.

Reynolds, J. (2022). *Ain't burned all the bright* (J. Griffin, Illus.). Atheneum/Caitlyn Dlouhy Books.

Rosenkranz, P. (2002). *Rebel visions: The underground comix revolution 1963–1975.* Fantagraphics Books.

Rowsell, J. (2020). "How emotional do I make it?": Making a stance in multimodal compositions. *Journal of Adolescent & Adult Literacy, 63*(6), 627–637.

Rozalski, M., Stewart, A., & Miller, J. (2010). Bibliotherapy: Helping children cope with life's challenges. *Kappa Delta Pi Record, 47*(1), 33–37.

Sadoski, M., & Paivio, A. (2013). *Imagery and text: A dual coding theory of reading and writing.* Routledge.

Savitz, R. S., & Stockwell, D. (2021). Student voice is power: Incorporating critical witness and testimony in middle-school classrooms. In J. DeHart, C. Meyer, & K. Walker (Eds.), *Connecting Theory and Practice in Middle School Literacy* (pp. 25–41). Routledge.

Schoonover, T., Hindman, M., Perryman, K., & Anderson, J. (2021). What is your superpower?: An elementary group using bibliotherapy with diverse fourth and fifth grade boys. *Journal of School Counseling, 19*(53), 1–30.

Searle, S. W. (2022). *The greatest thing.* First second.

Sell, C. (2018). *The cardboard kingdom.* Knopf Books for Young Readers.

Sell, C. (2020). *Doodleville.* Knopf Books for Young Readers.

Serafini, F. (2014). Exploring wordless picture books. *The Reading Teacher, 68*(1), 24–26.

Smoker, M.L., & Peeterse, N. (2022). *Thunderous* (D. Deforest, Illus.). Dynamite Entertainment.

Spiegelman, A. (1986). *Maus I: A survivor's tale: My father bleeds history.* Pantheon.

Stephens, O. (2021). *Artie and the wolf moon.* Graphic Universe.

Stevenson, N. (2015). *Nimona.* Quill Tree Books.

Stevenson, N., Watters, S., Ellis, G., & Allen, G.A. (2015). *Lumberjanes: Beware the kitten holy* (Vol. 1). BOOM! Box.

Telgemeier, R. (2019). *Guts.* Scholastic.

Telgemeier, R. (2020). *Smile.* Graphix.

Thomas, E. E. (2020). *The dark fantastic: Race and imagination from Harry Potter to the Hunger Games.* New York University Press.

Tobin, J. (2000). *"Good guys don't wear hats": Children's talk about the media.* Teachers College Press.

Tonatiuh, D. (2014). *Separate is never equal: Sylvia Mendez and her family's fight for desegregation.* Harry N. Abrams.

Tovani, C. (2000). *I read it, but I don't get it: Comprehension strategies for adolescent readers.* Stenhouse Publishers.

Tregonning, M. (2021). *Small things.* Pajama Press.

Tseng, C. I., & Bateman, J. A. (2018). Cohesion in comics and graphic novels: An empirical comparative approach to transmedia adaptation in *City of Glass. Adaptation, 11*(2), 122–143.

Vasquez, V., Janks, H., & Comber, B. (2019a). Critical literacy as a way of being and doing. *Language Arts, 96*(5), 300–311.

Vasquez, V., Janks, H., & Comber, B. (2019b). *Key aspects of critical literacy: An excerpt.* NCTE. https://ncte.org/blog/2019/07/critical-literacy/

Vaughan, B. K., Martin, M., & Vicente, M. (2018). *Barrier.* Image Comics.

Verrone, W. (2013). *Adaptation and the avant-garde: Alternative perspectives on adaptation theory and practice.* Bloomsbury Academic.

Walden, T. (2017). *Spinning.* First Second.

Walz, J. (2018). *Last pick.* First Second.

Wang, J. (2018). *The prince and the dressmaker.* First Second.

Wang, J. (2019). *Stargazing.* First Second.

Watt, M. (2006–2022). *Scaredy Squirrel.* Kids Can Press.

Whitlock, G. (2006). Autographics: The seeing "I" of the comics. *Modern Fiction Studies, 52*(4), 965–979.

Wohlwend, K. E. (2009). Damsels in discourse: Girls consuming and producing identity texts through Disney princess play. *Reading Research Quarterly, 44*(1), 57–83.

Yang, G. L. (2020). *Dragon hoops.* First Second.

Zinn, H., Konopacki, M., & Buhle, P. (2008). *A people's history of American empire: A graphic adaptation.* Metropolitan Books.

# Index

# Author

Jason D. DeHart has been reading comics since he was seven years old. His first issue was *Batman: Annual #12*. Since 2007, DeHart has worked as an educator, first in middle grades and then at the university level. He currently works with high school students in North Carolina. He earned a PhD in literacy studies at the University of Tennessee, Knoxville, in 2019, and his research has appeared in *The Journal of Adolescent & Adult Literacy, English Journal,* and *The Reading Teacher,* among other places. DeHart is a regular contributor at  *Edutopia* and *Middleweb,* and he has a number of edited and coedited books from Routledge, including *Connecting Theory and Practice in Middle School Literacy: Critical Conversations* with Carla Meyer and Katie Walker, *Teaching Challenged and Challenging Topics in Diverse and Inclusive Literature: Addressing the Taboo in the English Classroom* with Rachelle S. Savitz and Leslie Roberts, and a forthcoming two-volume project focused on arts-based research methods in education with Peaches Hash. DeHart has also edited work from IGI Global about film in the classroom, instruction with comics and graphic novels, phenomenological studies, religious diversity and equity, and digital literacy. He continues to highlight educators, authors, and creators on his podcast *Words, Images & Worlds.*

This book was typeset in AvenirNext, Myriad Pro, and Palatino by Barbara Frazier.

The typefaces used on the cover include Autobahn Stencil.

The book was printed on 50 lb., white offset paper.